T0008296

A Daily Word for Girls

FOR Girls

A 365-DAY
DEVOTIONAL

BroadStreet
PUBLISHING

BroadStreet Kids
Savage, Minnesota, USA
BroadStreet Kids is an imprint of BroadStreet Publishing Group, LLC.
Broadstreetpublishing.com

A Daily Word for Girls

9781424565917 (faux)
9781424565924 (e-book)

Devotional entries composed by Rachel Flores.

Typesetting and design by Garborg Design Works | garborgdesign.com

Editorial services by Carole Holdahl and by Michelle Winger | literallyprecise.com

Printed in China.

23 24 25 26 27 28 7 6 5 4 3 2 1

How can a young person keep their life pure? By living according to your word.

PSALM 119:9 NIRV

Introduction

Living for God can be hard. You probably hear many different messages about what is right and wrong, and that can be very confusing. God's Word is full of truth and life, and it can teach you how to make good decisions every day.

Spending time with God helps you to be a girl who is full of love, kindness, and joy. Each devotion in this book begins with one word for the day. Think about this word as you read the connected Bible verse, devotion, and question. Remember the word as you go about your day and see if it changes the way you think about things.

Let Jesus bring light and peace to your heart as you listen to his wisdom. When other people see his light shining in you, they will want it too!

JANUARY

God is our refuge and strength,
always ready to help
in times of trouble.

PSALM 46:1 NLT

PURPOSE

In Christ we were chosen to be God's people. God had already chosen us to be his people, because that is what he wanted. And God is the One who makes everything agree with what he decides and wants. We are the first people who hoped in Christ. And we were chosen so that we would bring praise to God's glory.

EPHESIANS 1:11-12 ICB

Why does it feel so good to be picked? It's amazing to be the first one off the line when they are picking sports teams, or to make the cut for the school drama, or to be called on when you confidently raise your hand in class. Did you know God chose you even before the world was created? He wanted you in his family and went to great lengths to make that happen.

You are accepted, wanted, chosen, and loved by the God of the universe. That truth will never change; you can never be cut from the team. What a beautiful promise! Remind yourself every day that this is who are; don't ever forget it.

How do you feel knowing you are accepted as God's child?

Decision

"If you refuse to serve the LORD,
then choose today whom you will serve.
But as for me and my family,
we will serve the LORD."

JOSHUA 24:15 NLT

Yolanda sat and listened to her Sunday school teacher intently. Her teacher was talking about each of us choosing to follow Jesus. She explained that following Jesus meant that we turn away from our sin, ask for forgiveness, and instead choose to live our lives according to God's Word. Yolanda felt puzzled. She had never considered that this was a decision she had to make for herself. Her mom and dad loved Jesus. They had always brought her to church, and everyone she knew seemed to love God too. Wasn't it enough that her whole family loved Jesus?

Shyly, she approached her teacher with her questions. Ms. Jane kindly explained that it doesn't matter if your mom and dad believe in Jesus. Each person must choose for themselves who they want to follow. Yolanda knew the answer to the question—she wanted to follow Jesus!

Have you chosen to follow Jesus?

Respected

An overseer must be so good that people cannot rightly criticize him. He must have only one wife. He must have self-control and be wise. He must be respected by other people and must be ready to help people by accepting them into his home. He must be a good teacher. He must not drink too much wine, and he must not be a man who likes to fight. He must be gentle and peaceful. He must not love money.

1 TIMOTHY 3:2-3 ICB

Serena sat in church with her parents. She didn't feel like going to Sunday school that morning. The pastor was talking about leadership, and she thought it was boring. Wasn't leadership basically just telling people what to do? As the pastor talked more about it, Serena realized that maybe it was more complicated than that.

Leadership is a serious job. There are many areas in life where you can be a leader, but the Bible specifically talks about what it means to be a leader in the church. God takes church leadership very seriously because he loves his children so much. He wants the people who teach them to be kind, qualified, and self-controlled. The best leaders are already respected by others because of how they live.

What Leaders do you look up to?

Brave

"Here's what I've learned through it all:
Don't give up; don't be impatient;
be entwined as one with the Lord.
Be brave and courageous, and never lose hope.
Yes, keep on waiting—for he will never disappoint you!"

PSALM 27:14 TPT

Janelle set down her book and stared off into space. What a story! She had just finished a biography about a famous female missionary. The missionary she had just read about had gone on a dangerous ship, all alone, to people she had never met, and she faced many hard things. Janelle couldn't ever imagine such a thing. She was afraid to cross the street without her sister! She wondered if she would ever be brave.

Just then, her sister came into the kitchen. When she saw what Janelle was reading, she asked her how she liked it. Janelle told her how she felt, and her sister gave her some wise advice. "Sometimes being brave doesn't mean you feel ready. It means you do it even if you feel scared. You pray, you ask God to give you courage, you remember that he will never leave you, and then you do it no matter what your feelings are."

When do you feel most brave?

Stay

"Remain in me, and I will remain in you.
No branch can produce fruit alone.
It must remain in the vine.
It is the same with you.
You cannot produce fruit alone.
You must remain in me."

JOHN 15:4 ICB

Has the Bible ever seemed impossible to you? From the Ten Commandments to the different lists in the New Testament, there are so many instructions on what to do. Being kind, loving, and patient, can sometimes feel overwhelming. How's a girl supposed to do them all?

Thankfully, we don't have to do it on our own. Just like fruit grows on a tree, these characteristics will grow in your life if you do one thing—remain in Jesus. Take the time to get to know him, listen to his Word, and let the Holy Spirit change your life. Without the power of the Spirit, we can't grow good fruit. If we stay close to Jesus, however, suddenly it won't be as hard to be loving or patient. The Holy Spirit will empower us to do those things!

How can you stay close to Jesus?

Appropriate

Everyone enjoys giving great advice.
But how delightful it is to say the right thing
at the right time!

PROVERBS 15:23 TPT

Do you know someone who talks all the time? Maybe it's hard to have a conversation with them because you feel like you can't get a word in! Perhaps that person is you! Just because we think something, doesn't mean it needs to be said. It isn't always appropriate. It is good discipline to learn when to speak and when to remain silent. Listening to others is a skill we want to learn. When we practice listening to others, it shows we care and value what they have to say. When we say whatever pops into our minds, we lack self-control, and sometimes our words can be hurtful.

Today, try to think about what you are saying before you say it. Try to practice truly listening to others and showing them the love of Jesus by letting his Holy Spirit guide the things you say.

What would practicing self-control look like for you today?

Faith

Faith means being sure of the things we hope for.
And faith means knowing that something is real
even if we do not see it.

HEBREWS 11:1 ICB

There are many things in this life that we don't understand.
Consider how complicated cellphones are. How can you pick
up a cellphone, put in a number, and talk to someone on the
other side of the country? There are so many questions to ask
about the world, and we will never be able to comprehend it all.

We often display faith by using things we don't understand.
In fact, even something as simple as sitting in a chair shows
faith; you trust that the chair won't break under you. Faith in
Jesus is like this. We can't see him, but we have faith that he
will do the things he promised and that we can put our
hope in him.

Do you believe Jesus is real and will do what he has promised?

CharacteR

I heard a voice from heaven, as the voice of many waters, and
as the voice of a great thunder: and I heard the voice
of harpers harping with their harps.

REVELATION 14:2 NIRV

Have you ever seen a sight so beautiful you wanted to
capture it in a photo or with words, yet you couldn't? The
picture could not adequately capture the beauty, and no
words could describe it properly. Maybe it was the colors of
a sunset or the vastness of the ocean. Whatever it was, you
really had to experience it yourself in order to understand.

John, the writer of the book of Revelation, had a vision of
heaven and many things that would happen at the end of
time, and boy, did he have a hard time describing them! He
saw Jesus in all his glory and heard his voice—the character
of Jesus all in one place was so powerful and amazing, John
could hardly find the words to describe him. We will see for
ourselves one day!

What chaRacteR quaLity do you Love Most about God?

Excited

I'm asking the LORD for only one thing.
Here is what I want.
I want to live in the house of the LORD
all the days of my life.
I want to look at the beauty of the LORD.
I want to worship him in his temple.

PSALM 27:4 NIRV

Dia leapt up and down with joy. Finally, after marking off the days on her calendar, the day had come. It was theme park day! Everyone who had gotten good grades would go on a special field trip to the local theme park. Dia had never been before, and she worked so hard this year to make the proper grades. She dreamed of cotton candy, fast rides, the waterpark, and best of all, her close friend was going too. It was going to be the perfect day!

The excitement that Dia felt about going to the theme park pales in comparison to the longing David felt to worship God in his temple. Does this sound weird to you, being so excited to go to church? David knew that time spent with God was the sweetest, best reward ever.

HOW CAN YOU CREATE A LONGING IN YOUR HEART TO BE WITH GOD?

Authority

You will know that God's power is very great for us who believe. That power is the same as the great strength God used to raise Christ from death and put him at his right side in heaven. God made Christ more important than all rulers, authorities, powers, and kings. Christ is more important than anything in this world or in the next world.

EPHESIANS 1:19-21 ICB

Do you like superhero movies? In every popular superhero film, there is always a bad guy wanting to have the most power in the world. Through a lot of battles, the superheroes usually win. These are great fiction stories, but what if I told you there is a real battle between good and evil?

Since the beginning of time, there has been a battle between those who follow God and those who want to be God. Satan wants to keep as many people away from knowing God as possible. The battle has already been told in the Bible, and God wins because he has the ultimate authority! If you side with Jesus, you are on the winning side. Jesus is the greatest superhero of them all, saving the whole world from the worst bad guys.

Whose authority do you submit to?

Empathy

Be joyful with those who are joyful.
Be sad with those who are sad.

ROMANS 12:15 NIRV

The two girls sat on the stairs, not saying a word. Bekah had shared with Tamira about how her grandpa had gotten sick and passed away. Tamira didn't know what to say, but she knew that being with her friend was the best thing she could do. She gently put her arm around Bekah. Whenever Bekah wanted to talk, Tamira listened. When her aunt had died, her mom said the most important thing other people did was come and sit with her.

Jesus did this in the Bible. When others were sad, he comforted them. Tamira knew that simply being with her friend would be showing her the love of Jesus. Just like the two friends experienced, the Bible asks us to be happy with those who are happy, and to be sad with those who are sad. This is called showing empathy, and it is a way we can show the love of Jesus.

How can you help a friend through a hard time?

EMPOWERED

"Thomas, now that you've seen me, you believe. But there
are those who have never seen me with their eyes but have
believed in me with their hearts, and they will be
blessed even more!"

JOHN 20:29 TPT

Thomas had his doubts. He had followed Jesus for three
years. He studied under him, served him, and lived with
him. Jesus had taught many things, some of which Thomas
understood and some he didn't. He had expected Jesus to
take over the Roman Empire right then, freeing the Jews
from those who hurt them. Instead, Thomas had watched
Jesus get arrested, stand trial, and die. How was any of this
part of the plan? His friends claimed Jesus had risen from
the dead. It was too unbelievable.

Thomas wanted to see with his own eyes. Jesus kindly
granted his request and let him feel the wounds in his hand
and sides. It was only then that Thomas believed. Do you
ever have doubts about who Jesus is? That's ok! Bring those
to him in prayer. When we believe without seeing, we are
blessed and empowered to continue in our faith.

What can you do to
strengthen your faith today?

Sure

Jesus said to her, "I am the resurrection and the life. Anyone who believes in me will live, even if they die. And whoever lives by believing in me will never die. Do you believe this?"

JOHN 11:25-26 NIRV

Mary and Martha were very sad. Their brother, Lazarus, had gotten very sick. Nothing had made him better. They knew their friend Jesus healed many people, and even though he was far away, they sent a message asking him to come. They were sure he could heal Lazarus and make it all better! But their brother got worse and worse. When Jesus finally came, they had buried Lazarus because he had died days before.

What Mary and Martha had to learn was that Jesus was God, and he was more powerful than death itself. They had never seen a dead person come to life, but Jesus told them to believe in him. He is the conquering King, the one who made a way for us to be with the Father forever. Spoiler alert: Jesus raised Lazarus from the dead, and they all rejoiced together.

What are you believing Jesus for today?

Dependable

A friend is always loyal,
and a brother is born to help in time of need.

PROVERBS 17:17 NLT

How would you define a friend? Is it someone who likes the same books and movies as you do? Is it someone who lives nearby, or is the same age as you? Those are all good, but that is not really what makes a friend.

The Bible gives us many explanations of what makes a good friend. Friends always love each other and help one another. They are dependable. Jesus used his life on earth to love and help others. He fed them, healed them, and taught them the ways of God. It makes him happy when we do what he did by loving and helping others. No matter how unimportant you may think you are, you can make a big difference by loving people like a dependable friend would.

How can you be a dependable friend?

Content

I know how to live when I am poor. And I know how to live when I have plenty. I have learned the secret of being happy at any time in everything that happens.

PHILIPPIANS 4:12 ICB

"Please! Just one more!" Jill looked at her dad with pleading eyes. They were walking past the toy aisle at the store. Jill had been collecting tiny dolls with rainbow hair for months. Even though she had bought one the last time they were there, she had seen another one that she didn't own. Her dad was ignoring her begging. Jill huffed. Her dad turned and said, "Jill, I wish you could be thankful and content for all that you already have." The look on his face told her the conversation was over. She followed him sadly, more upset about how she had acted than the fact that she couldn't have the doll.

To be content means to be satisfied. Paul wrote that no matter whether he was rich or poor, he was satisfied and happy because he had Christ. Just like Jill, we need to learn that we don't need more toys or things to make us happy. True happiness is only found in a relationship with Jesus.

How can you practice being content with what you have?

GENEROUS

Anyone who is kind to poor people lends to the LORD.
God will reward them for what they have done.

PROVERBS 19:17 NIRV

Kristina gazed around her room at all the new things she had gotten for Christmas. She ran her fingers across her new ski jacket. She had been blessed with many wonderful things. She couldn't help her mind from wandering back to the service on Sunday. A speaker had gotten up and talked about the homeless shelter just ten miles from where Kristina lived. There were people there who didn't have warm coats, and kids who didn't get extravagant gifts like she did.

She felt the tug of the Holy Spirit to give. She decided to do some extra chores that week and chose not to buy any snacks at school. She was going to take her other winter coat and boots over to the shelter later with the money she had saved. Kristina was acting generously toward others. Just because you are a kid, it doesn't mean you can't help.

How could you be generous toward the poor this week?

Grace

God continues to give us more grace.
That's why Scripture says,
"God opposes those who are proud.
But he gives grace to those who are humble."

JAMES 4:6 NIRV

Have you ever run out of a good thing? Those last few licks of an ice cream cone taste so good! The end of a good movie leaves you wanting more of the story. The last basketball game of the year gives both the team and the fans a feeling of completion. There is even the old saying that all good things must come to an end. Do you know something that's really good that never comes to an end?

The grace of God is one good thing that never, ever ends! Amazingly, the verse here says that God continues to give more. That means if grace were ice cream, he would keep scooping it up and you would never get a belly ache. If grace were a movie, the story would go on and on with a fresh round of popcorn. If grace were basketball season, you would play it all year around and not miss out on the satisfaction of a well-played season! God never runs out of grace, and he will never stop giving it to those who ask.

What do you find amazing about God's grace?

Pride

"Don't continue bragging. Don't speak proud words.
The Lord is a God who knows everything.
He judges what people do."

1 SAMUEL 2:3 ICB

Leah pulled down the screen with her finger once more to refresh it. Watching those hearts appear and the number of comments add up felt so good. She read through all the compliments on the gymnastics photo she posted on social media, relishing in each one. Two weeks later, Leah was still talking about the gold medal she got at State. She was still posting about how good it felt. The likes and comments slowed down, and her friends started avoiding her. Gently, Leah's coach pulled her aside to let her know the team was tired of hearing her brag. Leah felt crushed.

Then next night at the youth group, Pastor Bryan spoke about pridefulness. He said that when we find our worth in the things we do, we aren't finding our true worth in God. One of the symptoms of this is the need to brag and have others say nice things about you. Leah felt convicted and prayed right then that God would help her find her worth in him alone.

What do you find it hard not to brag about?

Legacy

We will not hide these truths from our children;
we will tell the next generation
about the glorious deeds of the LORD,
about his power and his mighty wonders.

PSALM 78:4 NLT

Imani looked around and smiled, enjoying the warm feeling in her heart. Her whole family had gathered for her great-grandmother's ninetieth birthday. Her parents, aunts, uncles, and cousins were eating, visiting, and laughing. After Grandpa Sam told another one of his classic jokes, everyone quieted down, and Aunt Jasmine began to sing. She was singing Grandmother Lois's favorite hymn, "What a Friend We Have in Jesus." One by one, the members of her family joined in, lifting their voices to God.

Imani listened for a while, feeling so grateful that her family loved Jesus. They shared Scriptures over meals, prayed for one another, and some even attended the same church. One of her best memories was of her grandma and aunts praying over her when she was very sick. Imani felt grateful for the legacy of her family that taught her about the one true God.

What have you LEARNED about God FROM SOMEONE OLDER THAN you?

Leader

Choose some capable men from among the people. Choose men who respect God and who can be trusted. They will not change their decisions for money. Make these men officers over groups of 1,000, 100, 50 and 10 people.

EXODUS 18:21 ICB

The Israelites had just been set free from slavery, and now they had a long journey ahead of them. They needed leaders to help get them through the journey. If someone didn't like the decision the leader made, they would try to pay the leader to influence them to change their minds. This is certainly not a good way to handle leadership!

In some ways, you are a leader as well. Maybe you lead a group at school, or you're the oldest of your siblings, or your friends are always looking to you to decide what to do. You can lead just one person or many. No matter how many you lead, what matters is how you lead. If you want to be a leader full of integrity, you can turn to God's Word for help.

How can you be a good leader?

Thoughtful

We who are strong must be considerate of those who are
sensitive about things like this. We must not just please
ourselves. We should help others do what is right and
build them up in the Lord. For even Christ didn't live
to please himself.

ROMANS 15:1-3 NLT

"All you think about is yourself!" Raina's sister yelled at her,
storming out the door. Though she didn't enjoy being yelled
at, Raina knew her sister was right. She felt that her sister
needed too much attention, and Raina just wanted to be
alone. Her sister made her tasks slower and harder. What's
wrong with thinking about myself? she thought as she sat
on her bed.

Beside her on the table sat the Bible that she had been given
by Ms. Rodan. She had read recently that Christ didn't live
to please himself. Ms. Rodan was always helping Raina
understand the verses, giving her a ride to church, sharing
snacks, and babysitting the girls while their mom worked. Ms.
Rodan was not selfish; she was thoughtful. Raina stood up
and went to find her sister. She needed to ask for forgiveness.
Her heart felt lighter as she walked out of the room.

What thoughtful thing could you do for someone today?

Healthy

Training the body has some value. But being Godly has
value in every way. It promises help for the life you
are now living and the life to come.

1 TIMOTHY 4:8 NIRV

Have you ever watched an adult work out? Maybe you think
it's silly that they have specific times to run, lift weights, or
do stretches. When you're a kid, running and jumping is
second nature! As we become adults, however, our bodies
change. Adults who want to keep their bodies healthy have
to make time for exercise.

Humans are made up of three parts. We have a body, soul,
and spirit. Running and stretching is great exercise for
your physical body, but the other two parts need attention
too. Reading your Bible and praying is vital for a healthy
soul. When you obey God's Word and spend time working
on your relationship with him, you exercise your spiritual
muscles. These different workouts will keep your whole
self healthy.

What healthy thing can you do this week?

Pleasant

The LORD is all I need.
He takes care of me.
My share in life has been pleasant;
my part has been beautiful.

PSALM 16:5-6 NCV

Life is pleasant when we know people care. You might be reminded of the soup your mom makes when you are sick, or the cool cloth she places on your forehead, or the soft touch of her hand when she checks for a fever. Maybe you think of your dad when he takes you out to eat, watches you play sports, or leaves a note in your lunchbox.

Whatever comes to your mind, it's feels good to be cared for. We need each other. Even more than our need for one another is our need for God. He has promised to take care of us in every way. He makes our lives pleasant and beautiful. If you don't know how you feel cared for, ask God to show you today!

How do you feel cared for?

Motivated

Everything a person does might seem pure to them.
But the LORD knows why they do what they do.

PROVERBS 16:2 NIRV

Stephanie had it all figured out. If she became good friends
with Helena, the good kid in class, then the teachers would
start to think she was a good kid too. She had a hard time
with her classes, and she often got into trouble. What she
really needed to do was change her image. Helena was kind
of cool, and she seemed to like Stephanie. What if she found
out the real reason Stephanie wanted to be friends?

It might be hard for others to figure out Stephanie's motives
for friendship, but it is not hard for God. He knows our hearts,
and the deep, real reasons we do the things we do. He knows
when we are being dishonest, or using someone, or lying. God
wants us to have pure hearts. Pray today that he will help you
to have motives that are true and honoring to him.

What does having pure motives look like to you?

Mindful

Why is man important to you?
Why do you take care of human beings?

PSALM 8:4 ICB

It was time for the end of year fair, and Jamie was so proud. She had worked incredibly hard building a robot of her own design. She programmed it and built it from scratch. Now was the time for her to show all her hard work, and her own creation! As the robot whizzed into action, Jamie beamed.

Have you ever created something you were so proud of? Like Jamie, you probably worked very hard and cared deeply about what happened to whatever you made. These feelings are small compared to how God feels about us. He fashioned and formed and breathed his own breath into us. He cares very much what happens to us! He is mindful of us.

How Mindful is God of you?

Moral

People shouted at him and made fun of him.
But he didn't do the same thing back to them.
When he suffered, he didn't say he would make them suffer.
Instead, he trusted in the God who judges fairly.

1 PETER 2:23 NIRV

Have you ever read the part of the Bible that tells about
the week of Jesus's death? He was treated horribly. He was
beaten several times, spit on, yelled at, cursed, stripped of
his clothes, deprived of sleep, and betrayed by his closest
friends. Yet even in the middle of these horribly hard things,
he didn't fight back. He didn't throw a punch or spit back. He
trusted that God would take care of him and bring fairness
in the end. That's hard!

Showing kindness to those who are not kind to you is
difficult. But this is the way of Jesus. His morals were perfect
and pure. The next time you face the temptation to be mean,
ask God to give you the strength to respond how he would.
Ask him to give you strong morals so you do the right thing
in the face of wrong things.

What do you think good morals are?

Positive

A cheerful heart makes you healthy.
But a broken spirit dries you up.

PROVERBS 17:22 NIRV

Have you ever heard the saying, "Laughter is good for the bones?" It's true! Laughter and joy are as good for you as vitamins are! Many people have been given the gift of joy. They love to tell good jokes, laugh until their bellies hurt, and have a smile that lights up the room. Did you know that these things are a gift from God?

God loves laughter and joy. He's given these blessings for both ourselves and for those around us. Many people in the world have forgotten this. You can be a bright light in others' lives with your positive attitude. Think today about someone who might need a good laugh.

How can you spread the gift of joy today?

Mature

We will speak the truth with love. We will grow up in every
way to be like Christ, who is the head. The whole body
depends on Christ. And all the parts of the body are joined
and held together. Each part of the body does its own work.
And this makes the whole body grow and be strong with love.

EPHESIANS 4:15-16 ICB

How does your hand know to turn the page, your eyes to
read the words, or your stomach to digest the breakfast you
ate? All these commands come from the command center of
your brain! Your brain is telling your body to do things, and
often you aren't even aware that it is doing so. What if, one
day, your mouth refused to open when your hand tried to
put food in it? That would be a disaster!

In the Bible, Christians are compared to parts of the body,
and Jesus is the head. He tells us how to live, what to do, and
how to grow into mature human beings. When one part of
the body chooses to disobey, it affects everyone!

How can you become more mature?

Patient

Patient endurance is what you need now,
so that you will continue to do God's will.
Then you will receive all that he has promised.

HEBREWS 10:36 NLT

3…2…1… Ashley jumped up and grabbed the microwave door before its last beep. She was so excited for the new cakes-in-a-cup her mom had found at the store. Just two minutes in the microwave and you have your very own small cake! As she grabbed her spoon, her grandma walked into the kitchen. "You know back in my day, we had to wait a long time for the cake to bake. You kids today are pretty lucky to get everything so quickly."

Ashley thought about how impatient she got even waiting for her two-minute cake. It reminded her that the Bible said she needs to have patience for most of the important things in life. Maybe her grandma could teach her about that. "Hey Grandma! Do you want to bake a real cake with me?" Grandma smiled, and as they mixed the ingredients, they talked about the good that was promised to them through Christ, and how patience was the ingredient to fully understand that message.

How can you show patience today?

Meaningful

Everything you speak to me is like joyous treasure,
filling my life with gladness.

PSALM 119:111 TPT

Many kids have a treasure box full of things they collect
from nature: seashells in dazzling colors, rocks that sparkle,
sticks shaped like toys, leaves, and flowers. The possibilities
are endless! The way God speaks to us and what he
communicates are much like that treasure box. It's important
to take note on what he says because that can bring great joy
into our lives.

God reveals himself to us in different ways: the natural
world, our conscience, the life of Jesus, and the Bible. Even
before we hear the gospel, it is written it on our hearts. God
speaks treasures of wisdom when we spend time with him.
Let's pay attention and collect the jewels he is handing out.

What treasures have you been collecting?

MENTOR

Follow my example,
as I follow the example of Christ.

1 CORINTHIANS 11:1 ICB

Do you know what it means to be a Christian? Christian means "little Christ." The early church was so dedicated to acting like Jesus that those around them gave them this name. That's exactly how it should be. As we learn more about the Word of God and who Jesus is, our lives should begin to look like his. We should respond in the ways he did, love like he does, and serve as he would. He is our greatest mentor.

There are many adults who began their Christian journey long ago and are further along the path than you may be. These believers can be helpful and encouraging. Pray that God will give you someone to mentor you in your faith.

Who can you learn more about Jesus from?

FEBRUARY

"Go and enjoy good food
and sweet drinks.
Send some to people who have none.
Today is a hold day to the Lord.
Don't be sad. The joy of the Lord
will make you strong."

NEHEMIAH 8:10 ICB

Honest

Kings are pleased when what you say is honest.
They value people who speak what is right.

PROVERBS 16:13 NIRV

"Have you brushed your teeth, Destiny?" Her mom called from the kitchen. "Yes, Mom!" The lie slipped easily off Destiny's tongue. Destiny hated brushing her teeth. The first time she lied to her mom about it, she felt really bad. The second time was easier, and now the words danced right out. In fact, Destiny almost believed them herself. Destiny's dad peeked his head out of the office. "I never heard the sink, and you haven't been in the bathroom." He frowned at her.

Busted! She tried to tell another lie. Destiny's dad knelt down and looked at her. "When you tell a little lie, it tears down the trust we have built with you, and we have to start over. It leads to more lies like a snowball rolling down a mountain." Destiny knew he was right. She wanted her parents' trust. Her dad showed her how to pray for forgiveness and turn from lying.

What do you need to be honest about?

INCREDIBLE

The sky was made at the LORD's command.
By the breath from his mouth, he made all the stars.

PSALM 33:6 NCV

The snow fell steadily through the night. When Shannon woke up, the world had turned into a beautiful snow globe. She hopped out of bed and pressed her nose against the window. A large ring of fog formed from her breath on the glass. She leaned back and drew a design in the fog before it faded away. As she ran downstairs, she paused to look out the hall window. It was covered in intricate designs of frost, like sketches from an incredible artist. Snow days felt so magical! After a warm breakfast, she put on her snow gear and bounded outside. She could see her breath in the cold air.

Shannon enjoyed all the beauty of a snow day. Her joy and acknowledging God are forms of worship. He created our beautiful, incredible world. Just like Shannon breathed and saw her breath, God breathed and created the stars! Enjoy some time outside today and thank God for his wonderful creation.

What incredible thing can you thank God for today?

Rejoice

Let the fields and everything in them show their joy.
Then all the trees of the forest will sing for joy.
They will sing before the Lord because he is coming.
He is coming to judge the world.
He will judge the world with fairness
and the nations with truth.

PSALM 96:12-13 ICB

Psalm 96 is like one big dance party for God. It talks about how we should praise God for his wonderful attributes like his strength and beauty. It tells us he will return and set things right, and that he will be a fair judge. It is not just us who are called to rejoice but all of nature too!

Imagine the trees singing, their leaves clapping and branches swaying. Imagine fields bursting forth with arrays of colorful flowers. The oceans roar out songs of praise to the Lord. If you listen, it's happening now. Our natural world knows who made it. It knows God is good and worthy of praise. Don't make the rocks cry out on their own. Lift your voice to God and rejoice in his goodness today!

How can you Rejoice today?

ANSWERS

Now we see but a faint reflection of riddles and mysteries
as though reflected in a mirror, but one day we will see
face-to-face. My understanding is incomplete now,
but one day I will understand everything, just as
everything about me has been fully understood.

1 CORINTHIANS 13:12 TPT

Do you like riddles? Here is an old one: Thirty white horses
stand on a red hill. First they champ, then they stamp, then
they stand still. Can you guess what the horses are? Teeth!
Riddles can be fun, but they can leave us guessing the
answer for hours. It's not supposed to be like that with God
and his love.

We live in a world still under the curse of sin, so the full
greatness of what it is like to be with God is not our current
reality. People still hurt each other, and bad things do
happen. Sickness and death are still part of our lives. But
one day, the answer to all these riddles will be given to us.
And most important of all, we will see Jesus face-to-face.
What a promise!

What would you like to ask God about?

Real

Stop telling lies.
Let us tell our neighbors the truth,
for we are all parts of the same body.

EPHESIANS 4:25 NLT

It is never good to lie no matter how tiny you think the lie is. The Bible is very clear that lying is bad, and in fact it is even one of the Ten Commandments. Whether you tell someone you didn't do something to save yourself from getting into trouble, or pretend something cool happened to you so other people think you are cool, or say someone doesn't have dirt on their face when they do; those are all lies.

This doesn't mean you need to point out every time someone's face is dirty, but if you are asked, it's your duty to kindly tell the truth. Always be real in the simple, little things as well as the big, hard things. This is the way Jesus wants us to walk.

How can you be real today?

Lively

Don't act thoughtlessly,
but understand what the Lord wants you to do.

EPHESIANS 5:17 NLT

Board games come with instructions that tell you how to play the game. You can, of course, take the pieces and put them where you want and do what you want with the instructions, but you won't enjoy the fullness of the game unless you follow the instructions. Life can be like that board game.

The Bible serves many different purposes. One of its purposes is to be a love letter from God. It tells us the story of how much God loves us and wants to make a way for us to be with him forever. There are also parts of the Bible that are like an instruction manual for life. You can do life your own way, but you will get a better understanding from God about how to live well straight from his Word.

What instructions are you asking God for right now?

ENDURE

The LORD is good. His faithful love continues forever.
It will last for all time to come.

PSALM 100:5 NIRV

Have you ever had a countdown calendar? Sometimes we countdown to important days, or maybe you have been counting down to the last day of school. It can seem like time is taking so long, but soon that event we are looking forward to will come. What does forever actually feel like? It's pretty mind-blowing to understand.

Did you know that God's love for you lasts that long? What a long time! There is nothing you can do to separate yourself from his love. No matter how much you mess up, his love always endures. That means is lasts through everything. It's never failing, and it's never changing. That's good news!

How do you feel knowing that God's love for you endures forever?

Steady

Watch where you're going!
Stick to the path of truth,
and the road will be safe and smooth before you.

PROVERBS 4:26 TPT

"It's called off-roading!" Jaylen's dad shouted as the car jostled and bumped down the made-up path. Jaylen couldn't respond; she was too busy trying to stay in her seat. Her little brother, though, had his opinion. "Maybe we should have stuck to the actual road!" Suddenly, they heard a pop. Off-roading might not have been a good idea after all.

If you think about life as a path, the way of God is the smooth, steady road. This doesn't mean that life with Jesus will be easy, but it will be the best way to go. Following your own desires and sins is like going off the path, bumping and jostling until finally you get a flat tire. That's no way to travel! Stick to the ways of Christ on your life journey.

How can you stay on the steady path of truth?

IMPROVE

Let us do all we can to live in peace.
And let us work hard to build up one another.

ROMANS 14:19 NIRV

Conflict between siblings is as old as the first family—Cain and Abel in the book of Genesis had a lot of fights! What can we do to improve the peace between our siblings and friends? First, we need to respect everyone as being made in the image of God. When we start to see them as God's creation, it changes the way we treat them.

Next, we must learn how to say what we feel and ask for forgiveness when we've hurt others. We have to be willing to admit when we are wrong or even partially wrong. Many conflicts come from assuming that someone else knows how you feel even if you've never told them. These are just a few ways to improve your peace.

How can you improve a tough situation you are in?

Focus

"The one who endures to the end will be saved."

MATTHEW 24:13 NLT

Kassidy listened to the steady rhythm of the music in her headphones. It helped her to keep focused. She was on her first hiking trip with her friends, Sally and Macy, and their mom. She had never hiked this far before, but the promise of the view from the top of the mountain kept her going. Once before she had tried to go hiking, and she remembered how much she whined about the walking and the bugs. Her dad had gotten so tired of it they ended up turning around before they even got to the waterfall. This time would be different. She would make it to the end.

Our Christian walk can be compared to a hike. It's hard at times, but those who keep focused on Jesus and keep going will have a great reward in the age to come.

What are you focusing on right now?

Reward

We must not become tired of doing good.
We will receive our harvest of eternal life at the right time.
We must not give up!

GALATIANS 6:9 ICB

Dad laid down his spade. "Finished!" He looked triumphantly over at his three daughters. "Thanks for all your hard work!" The Garcia family had decided to plant a community garden. They planned it out, ordered the seeds, cleared the plot of land behind their house, and built a fence. The list of work went on and on. Mr. Garcia said it was a family project, so everyone in the family needed to help. It was hard work, and Monica often thought about doing everything but working on the garden. She never gave up, and when August finally came, vegetables and flowers were the reward.

Monica felt proud of all they had accomplished. The best part was seeing the families who couldn't afford groceries come and get their free, fresh vegetables right from that community garden. It felt good to work hard and give to others. It won't always be easy to do the right thing, but God promises great rewards for those who continue to do good works.

What are you working hard for right now?

Stable

From long ago no one has ever heard of a God like you.
No one has ever seen a God besides you,
who helps the people who trust you.

ISAIAH 64:4 NCV

Cassie knew she could rely on her dad. He was always there when she needed him. If she had a problem, the first thing she did was talk to her dad. Cassie knew she could trust her dad because he had proven she could. He had always been stable. He wasn't perfect, but he never let her down when it counted.

It is good to have people in your life who you can trust. But no matter how great they are, they aren't perfect. God will never break your trust. He is trustworthy. This means he will do what he says, and you can rely on him.

Do you know you can always rely on God?

Significant

"Do not be afraid. I will set you free.
I will send for you by name.
You belong to me."
ISAIAH 43:1 NIRV

Diana excitedly dumped her mailbox of cards onto the kitchen table. At their class Valentine's Day party, the students had exchanged candies and cards. She sorted through the pile, putting all the candy together and reading each card. Most of the cards were similar, but one stood out. It was handmade and beautifully decorated with her name on the front. When she flipped it over, she saw a puzzle that led to a scavenger hunt to be done right in her own home.

Diana followed all the clues to a bowl full of her favorite candy and a big vase of beautiful flowers. She felt significant and loved. Just then, Dad came around the corner and gave her a hug. The personal card and gifts were from him. Diana felt so special. God knows you by name. He loves you deeply and personally. Never forget you are chosen, special, and loved by the King.

Do you feel significant to God?

Love

Most importantly, love each other deeply, because love will
cause people to forgive each other for many sins.

1 PETER 4:8 NCV

Erin didn't know what it was about her little sister that made
her so angry. They were five years apart, and it seemed
almost impossible to get along. No one else made her feel
this way. She didn't want to be angry, and she tried hard
to control herself. She often found herself needing to ask
for forgiveness. Every time she asked, her sister graciously
forgave her. Her mom and dad also helped her and forgave
her each time she apologized. It was wonderful to be loved in
this way.

There isn't a single person on earth who is perfect. Everyone
makes mistakes every day. Even when the people we love
mess up, we should continue to love them. Jesus didn't
wait for us to be perfect to love us. He extends love and
forgiveness to everyone who asks.

Aren't you glad that you are loved by God even though you make mistakes?

Reliable

Teach those who are rich in this world not to be proud and not to trust in their money, which is so unreliable. Their trust should be in God, who richly gives us all we need for our enjoyment.

1 TIMOTHY 6:17 NLT

As a kid, when you need something, you turn to the person who takes care of you. Your parents, grandparents, foster parents, aunts, and uncles are the people placed in your life to take responsibility for you. They make sure you have all you need and even many of the things you simply want. You trust them to do this for you, and they are usually reliable.

God is the caretaker of all who trust in him. He will provide everything they need. As a child of God, you can trust him to never abandon you. When you have a need, bring it to God in prayer before you start counting your pennies. Let him know that you trust in his goodness to take care of you.

Who do you find to be the most reliable in your life?

SeRious

The time is near when all things will end. So think clearly
and control yourselves so you will be able to pray.

1 PETER 4:7 NCV

All good things must come to an end. Even the world as
we know it will one day end. The good news is that when it
does, Jesus will return and welcome into his kingdom those
who trusted in him. In this verse, we are given very specific
instructions about how to act. It doesn't say to start stocking
up on food, or to try to figure out what day it will be when
everything ends. It simply says to make sure you're focused
enough to pray. Take it seriously.

God is in control of our whole world. We don't need to take
that control away from him. Our task is to simply trust in him.
You can spend your time praying for those who don't know
Christ, praying for Jesus to come soon, and worshiping God
for your relationship with him. He will take care of the rest.

How do you feel about Jesus coming back?

Civil

Let the words you speak always be full of grace.
Learn how to make your words what people want to hear.
Then you will know how to answer everyone.

COLOSSIANS 4:6 NIRV

Haddy walked into the kitchen. She slid into her seat at the island, listening in on the conversation between her sister Lily and their mom. They were discussing Lily's favorite book. Haddy spoke up, mentioning a part that she liked, even though she had never read the book. Lily, annoyed, quickly reminded her she couldn't read. Haddy was stung by her comment, and her mom quickly jumped in. "Lily, how you speak matters."

Even if the words we are saying are true, how we say them matters a lot. It's called your tone of voice. You can say the same thing with different tones of voice, either annoyed or kind, and the message behind your words will be clear by that tone. When you are speaking to others, think before you say any words and make sure you check your tone. This is called being civil.

What can you do to make sure you think before you speak?

BRilliant

What he does is glorious and splendid.
His goodness continues forever.

PSALM 111:3 ICB

If you ever want your mind blown, just take a minute to consider outer space. Did you know that our sun weighs over three hundred thousand times more than the earth? Or that scientists believe there are more stars in the universe than there are grains of sand on our planet? Think about that!

These facts and more will leave your head spinning and hopefully move your heart to be in awe of the one who made it all—God! He is so powerful and mighty; he has created brilliant things like the sun and the stars. The Bible tells us that he has a name for each of those stars. That's a lot of names! Praise God today for how infinitely amazing he is.

What fact about God's brilliant creation have you learned recently?

Trustworthy

You will keep in perfect peace
all who trust in you,
all whose thoughts are fixed on you!

ISAIAH 26:3 NLT

Sometimes our brains feel like the wild, wild west—so many thoughts are roaming around, doing whatever they want! Our thinking may be out of control, and all our thoughts are not good. The negative things people say, and our own self-doubt, can gallop around in our heads without any mercy!

Bring a new sheriff to town and drive out all those bad thoughts: fix your mind on Jesus. If you are feeling down about a certain part of yourself, find a Bible verse that tells you the truth. Memorize it. Tell Jesus exactly what thoughts are bothering you. Sing a worship song to help bring your mind back to the wondrous truth of who God is. He is the one you can truly trust.

How can you fix your thoughts on God today?

Unafraid

Anyone who shows respect for the LORD has a strong tower.
It will be a safe place for their children.

PROVERBS 14:26 NIRV

If you've ever been to the coast, you may have seen a lighthouse. Usually, they are tall and cylinder-shaped. At the top of lighthouses are lights that can penetrate through the thick fog that often comes on the sea, and they can therefore guide ships safely along the shoreline. The lighthouse represents a safe place for those who sail on the sea. Imagine trying to navigate through a thick fog. The piercing light of the lighthouse brings great relief to those during a storm.

God is a lighthouse for us. He is a strong tower and a piercing, guiding light when things are foggy. Sometimes we don't know what to do in life's circumstances. We feel like we can't see, and we are afraid. God is there to guide us through. He will never let us crash.

What fears can you give to God today?

Steadfast

They will not live in fear or dread of what may come,
for their hearts are firm, ever secure in their faith.

PSALM 112:7 TPT

In northern California, there is a forest in which the tallest trees grow. These trees are mostly redwoods, and they can reach almost four hundred feet in height! Interestingly enough, hundreds of feet up in the trees the branches grow so closely together that animals can live in the canopy, almost like a second floor. The animals that live their whole lives way up there have everything they need, wonderfully provided by the redwood tree canopy. The trees are their steadfast source of life.

Jesus is our source of hope. Every good thing he has promised in the Bible is coming true. Just like the creatures in the tree, you can rely on God to give you everything you need. There's no need to try to look elsewhere. Stay steadfast in your faith.

How has God been your steadfast hope?

Enough

"You must not covet your neighbor's house. You must not covet your neighbor's wife, male or female servant, ox or donkey, or anything else that belongs to your neighbor."

EXODUS 20:17 NLT

Janey was half-listening as she checked off boxes in her head. She didn't want a different house, she was far too young for marriage, and no one she knew had servants, oxen, and donkeys. She was in the clear. Ms. Turner stopped reading straight from the Bible and looked at her class. "Class, how many of you think this applies to you?" Almost everyone raised their hand except Janey. The teacher went on.

The Bible lists things that were common for people to desire at the time it was written. This list is not complete. It's very easy for us to look at those around us and desperately want something they have: their phone, their great parents, their talent, or anything at all! Make your own list. God asks us to be content. He is more than enough.

Do you have enough?

Unique

You created the deepest parts of my being.
You put me together inside my mother's body.

PSALM 139:13 NIRV

When someone wants to build a grand structure like the
Empire State Building or the Eiffel Tower, it all starts with
something called a blueprint. This is a special drawing that
shows the detailed plan for that building. The blueprint of
you is called DNA, and it's the unique code of how you are
made. Your eye color, hair color, and every other detail of
you is written in that DNA code. God put it all in there. Each
person has their own unique DNA code.

All your cells follow this code and make up one unique you.
That's amazing! If you ever feel like you don't stand out or
you're unloved, remember how special and unique you are
to God. He made only one you, and he loves you exactly the
way you are.

How are you unique in your family?

Charity

God supplies seed for the person who plants. He supplies bread for food. God will also supply and increase the amount of your seed. He will increase the results of your good works.

2 CORINTHIANS 9:10 NIRV

Florence grew up in a small town in the United States. She lived with her parents and four siblings. She was blessed with three meals daily, as well as snacks, clean water to drink, and a closet full of clothes. She just finished fourth grade and loved reading mystery novels. Florence and her parents would not say they are rich, but compared to the rest of the world, Florence's family is in the top ten percent.

God supplies so we can be generous. The whole point in having more than enough is so we can generously share. In doing so, we show God's love to those who have less. If your life sounds a lot like Florence's, talk to your parents today about ways that you could give to those who don't have as much as you do.

How can you be generous with what you have?

HELPFUL

"It is not good for the man to be alone.
I will make a helper who is just right for him."

GENESIS 2:18 NLT

These are the words God spoke before he made a woman.
Some may think that because this word helper is used, that
women are less important than men. That's not true at all! In
fact, this word is the same word that is used to describe the
Holy Spirit. The Holy Spirit is equal in the Trinity to both
Jesus and to the Father. He is just as much God as the other
parts of the Trinity.

A helper is no less important than the person being helped.
In fact, being helpful is a strength that is very much needed.
Everyone is made in the image of God. Being a helper is an
honor. Today let's thank God for the special roles he gives us,
for making us in his image, and for girls being honored and
loved as part of God's creation.

How can you be a good helper today?

Eager

You should continue following the teachings you learned.
You know they are true, because you trust those who
taught you. Since you were a child you have known the
Holy Scriptures which are able to make you wise. And that
wisdom leads to salvation through faith in Christ Jesus.

2 TIMOTHY 3:14-15 NCV

Have you ever been on a scavenger hunt for treasure? It's
so fun! Following the clues until you find the prize is very
exciting. It can even be fun to pretend that you are an
explorer or pirate when searching for the treasure.

Reading the Bible and knowing God's Word is like a treasure
hunt as well. The difference is the prize that you get in the
end is wisdom! Wisdom is the ability to discern what is
right and true and then choosing to do it. We gain so much
wisdom from the Word of God. Wisdom leads us to know
and believe in Jesus, and that's the greatest treasure any
person could find!

How eager are you for the greatest treasure?

Self-control

Better to be patient than powerful;
better to have self-control than to conquer a city.

PROVERBS 16:32 NLT

Have you read the story of Joseph in the Bible? You can find it at the end of the book of Genesis. Joseph was treated very poorly by his brothers; they actually sold him into slavery! Later in his life, Joseph became a very high official in the land of Egypt. Next to the Pharaoh, he was the most powerful man in the country. Years later, when Joseph's brothers come to Egypt to look for food, he had the perfect opportunity to get back at them. He could have treated them the way they had treated him, but instead of wanting revenge, Joseph showed grace and self-control.

God wants us to show self-control, but we can't do it alone. He promised to give us the power to do so. When your emotions or actions are out of control, pray, and ask the Holy Spirit to fill you with the control you need to act according to God's Word.

How can you show self-control today?

Considerate

God's grace has been given to me. So here is what I say to every one of you. Don't think of yourself more highly than you should. Be reasonable when you think about yourself. Keep in mind the faith God has given to each of you.

ROMANS 12:3 NIRV

You know what is a fascinating part of your body? Your nose! It smells, helps us breathe, and is rather handy if you wear glasses! Noses aren't good for looking down on other people. It's called turning your nose at people when you think and act like you are better than them.

The Bible tells us to treat others in the way we would like to be treated—being considerate. This involves not acting like we are the smartest, prettiest, richest, or whatever "est" we may think we are. Instead, we need to find ways to lift others up and be kind to them. This is the example Jesus gave us, and we should follow his example every time.

What makes a person considerate?

MARCH

"Don't worry, because I am with you.
Don't be afraid, because I am your God.
I will make you strong and will help you.
I will support you with my
right hand that saves you."

ISAIAH 41:10 ICB

Polite

Tell them not to speak evil things against anyone. Remind
them to live in peace. They must consider the needs of
others. They must always be gentle toward everyone.

TITUS 3:2 NIRV

Sometimes our mouths can get us into big trouble! How
is it that such a tiny part of our bodies can stir up so many
issues? Over and over again, the way we speak is addressed
in Scripture. The old saying about sticks and stones hurting
but words cannot is simply not true. Words stick, and they
cut, and they can destroy lives. That is why the Bible tells us
to be careful about the things we say.

Words can be used for life or death. We need to encourage
other people, be kind to them, and use gentle words. Evil
words can hurt, sarcastic words can sting, and lies and
rumors can damage relationships forever. These are just a few
examples of ways you can use your words in opposite ways.

How will you choose to use your words today?

Potential

Jesus has the power of God, by which he has given
us everything we need to live and to serve God.
We have these things because we know him.
Jesus called us by his glory and goodness.

2 PETER 1:3 NCV

"It's too hard!" Jessica whined again. Her dad had asked
her to bring her sister's motorized scooter up the hill to the
garage, but she could not get it to budge. She knew it had the
potential to move, but she didn't know that with the motor
off, the wheels lock up. Her dad walked down the hill toward
her, took the scooter and flipped on the switch. He handed
it back to Jessica, and suddenly she didn't even need to push;
she just flew straight up that hill!

Without the power of the Holy Spirit, we can't do the things
God asks us to do. We have potential, but we have to ask
the Holy Spirit to help us. Then it becomes easier. Don't try
to force out good fruit and push your way uphill with good
deeds. Instead, rely on the power of the Holy Spirit.

What Potential do you have that needs a kickstart from the Holy Spirit?

Pure

These troubles come to prove that your faith is pure.
This purity of faith is worth more than gold, which can be
proved to be pure by fire but will ruin. But the purity of your
faith will bring you praise and glory and honor when
Jesus Christ is shown to you.

1 PETER 1:7 NCV

If you've ever watched an old western or pirate movie, you know that the main characters are usually after one thing—gold. Did you know, however, that in order for gold to be worth something, it needs to be purified first? Fire heats the gold up to such high temperatures that it separates the dirt and other debris from the gold, leaving only pure gold. That's something they don't really show you in old movies!

In the same way, difficult times in our lives can be like the fire that will reveal to us what we truly have faith in. A pure faith is in Jesus alone as we rely only on him. Those hard times can show us whether we are putting our faith in ourselves, in others, in the ways of this world, or in the pure ways of God.

What do you need God to purify in you?

Responsive

Stay alert! Watch out for your great enemy, the devil.
He prowls around like a roaring lion,
looking for someone to devour.

1 PETER 5:8 NLT

Have you ever watched a show about lions? Lions stalk their
prey, watching and waiting for the perfect moment to attack.
The prey often doesn't even realize the lion is there until it is
too late. The lion springs from their hiding place, knocking
over their prey. Interestingly enough, lions are not the fastest
of animals and do not enjoy a long chase, so it is the element
of surprise that they use to capture their dinner.

The Bible tells us that Satan is like a lion, waiting to pounce
on us and devour us. We are constantly tempted to sin and
disobey God. But the Bible promises that God will give us a
way to escape—a way to run! We don't have to give in to sin.

What temptations are you asking Jesus to help you with?

Quiet

I am standing in absolute stillness,
silent before the one I love,
waiting as long as it takes for him to rescue me.
Only God is my Savior, and he will not fail me.

PSALM 62:5 TPT

Imagine you are in a room, and it's full of people. You want to hear what your dad has to say because he promised you some really great things earlier. But even with him right next to you, everyone talking around you drowns out his voice. You can't hear one word, and because of that you miss out on his great promises. How disappointing!

We live in a noisy world. Things like TV, radio, phones, social media, and video games keep our ears plugged with noise and busyness. Is God going to shout over all that noise to speak to us, and would we even hear him if he did? It's good to take time to be quiet and listen for the voice of God. We can hear what he has to say if we turn off all the outside noise and listen.

Can you be quiet before God today?

Heir

Since we are his true children, we qualify to share all his treasures, for indeed, we are heirs of God himself. And since we are joined to Christ, we also inherit all that he is and all that he has. We will experience being co-glorified with him provided that we accept his sufferings as our own.

ROMANS 8:17 TPT

Have you ever been to a family reunion and been introduced as someone's daughter, niece, or granddaughter? Maybe at school you are known as someone's little sister. These labels identify you by who you belong to, and who your family is. Every Christian is a child of God. What a title to be known by!

Because you are a child of a God, you share in the gifts that he gives his family. You get these things not by any hard work or anything you do on your own. They are all free for his children. What a great honor to be an heir of God!

Are you known by others as a child of God? Do your actions reflect his Word?

Humble

Always be humble and gentle. Be patient with each other,
making allowance for each other's faults because of your
love. Make every effort to keep yourselves united in the
Spirit, binding yourselves together with peace.

EPHESIANS 4:2-3 NCV

Do you like playing with balloons? They are a great, simple
toy for all ages. You can hit them around like a ball, use them
as decoration, draw on them, and many other cool things. A
balloon usually needs air or water to be fun. Each time you
put air or water in it, the balloon gets bigger, but if you fill it
up too much, what happens? Your balloon will pop.

We can be like balloons sometimes. We get all puffed up with
pride and then we think we are better than others. Maybe we
think we are the best singer, the fastest runner, the prettiest,
or the smartest. Comparing ourselves to others and filling up
on our pride is just like blowing up the balloon too much—
one day it will pop! The Bible tells us to be humble instead.

How are you practicing humility in your life?

Drift

Don't let me drift toward evil
or take part in acts of wickedness.
Don't let me share in the delicacies
of those who do wrong.

PSALM 141:4 NLT

Have you ever been in a lazy river? They are a favorite attraction at many waterparks. People enjoy sitting in water tubes, drifting along the river at a slow pace. They aren't trying to move toward anything. The river does the work, simply carrying them along. This is an example of drifting. You aren't trying to get anywhere.

Our world is a fallen world, meaning that there is sin all around us. To walk in the way of Jesus instead of living as the world does is like trying to swim upstream. To follow the way of sin can be as simple as letting the river carry you along. God gives us the strength to not drift with the evil of the world, but to boldly swim upstream in his will.

What would it look like for you to swim upstream instead of drifting?

Knowledge

I pray that your love will grow more and more. And let it be based on knowledge and understanding. Then you will be able to know what is best. Then you will be pure and without blame for the day that Christ returns.

PHILIPPIANS 1:9-10 NIRV

Think of someone you love deeply. Write down some of your favorite things about them. You could probably fill a whole notebook with memories, facts, what they like and don't like. That's because your love for them has grown through knowing them.

It is the same with God. We can't say we really love God without getting to know him more. The more we get to know him, the more there is to love! The best way to get to know God is through his Word. Find out what the Bible says about his character. He is gentle, kind, loving, and full of mercy. What a wonderful friend we have in Jesus!

What do you know about God's character?

INSPiRation

The Lord has filled Bezalel with the Spirit of God. The Lord
has given Bezalel the skill, ability and knowledge to do all
kinds of work. He is able to design pieces to be made of
gold, silver and bronze.

EXODUS 35:31-32 ICB

When people say that you can serve God, what kind of
things come to your mind? Do you think about being a
worship leader? Or possibly you consider being a pastor who
teaches and preaches. How else can we serve God? What if
we don't want to preach, or we can't sing, or we don't know
how to play an instrument?

Our God gives us a wide variety of gifts so we can serve him.
Bezalel was given the gift of design. He worked with different
types of metals, and he used this craft to glorify God. How
neat! Creating art, making music, writing, building, helping
others, working with paper, playing sports, dancing, or
watching children in the nursery—there are just so many
ways to serve God!

What are your special gifts?

Needed

Some parts of the body that seem weakest and least important are actually the most necessary. So, God has put the body together such that extra honor and care are given to those parts that have less dignity. This makes for harmony among the members, so that all the members care for each other.

1 CORINTHIANS 12:24-25 NLT

Did you know that all believers worldwide are called the body of Christ? The Bible tells us that Jesus is the head of the body, and those of us who have faith in him make up the body. If you think about the human body, you will quickly conclude that every part is needed. Arms have their role just like stomachs and ears do. There are also the parts that work behind the scenes, like the kidneys and the joints. What's important is that the whole body works together.

Unity in the body of Christ is also important. Every gift is needed, and every believer has an important role to play. It is beautiful when the body of Christ works together to bring glory to God.

What is your role in the body of Christ?

WORTHLESS

Not only those things, but I think that all things are worth nothing compared with the greatness of knowing Christ Jesus my Lord. Because of him, I have lost all those things, and now I know they are worthless trash. This allows me to have Christ.

PHILIPPIANS 3:8 NCV

Aaliyah looked at the trophy in her hand. She felt a rush of pride in her chest whenever she looked at it. It's not that the trophy itself was so amazing, but it was what it stood for. She had finished the five-kilometer race at her school. It was a hard race and not everyone had completed it. The trophy represented the fact that she had worked so hard and never gave up. That was meaningful to her. The hard work was worth it.

Paul compares our Christian life to a race. It's not the person who is the fastest who wins, but all who endure to the end get the trophy. Instead of chasing after the worthless things in the world, stick with what is worthy—Jesus!

What do you find value in?

PERMANENT

LORD, remind me how brief my time on earth will be.
Remind me that my days are numbered—
how fleeting my life is.

PSALM 39:4 NLT

Brianna bowed her head with the rest of the people in
church for a prayer. Everyone was dressed in black. She
resisted the urge to stare at the coffin in front of her. In it
was her dearly missed grandmother. Death is so horrible!
she thought. Later, her Aunt Titia put her arm around her.
Aunt Titia always knew what to say. She saw Brianna's tears,
knelt down, and took her chin in her hands. She reminded
Brianna that though they all missed Grandma very much,
she loved Jesus, so they could hold onto the promise that she
was with him in heaven.

As believers, we will be reunited with those who have gone
to heaven before us. Our lives on earth may be long or
short, and it is painful when our loved ones die, but those
who trust in Jesus will be with him forever. So, we are really
saying "see you later" instead of goodbye.

How is the sting of death taken away in light of this good news?

MERCY

Have mercy on me, O God, because of your unfailing love.
Because of your great compassion,
blot out the stain of my sins.

PSALM 51:1 NLT

Karina stood patiently by the dryer as her mom explained how to do the laundry. As a new ten-year-old, it was now one of her chores to do her own laundry. Her mom explained how to turn on the washer, and then started going through each product and how it was to be used.

"This is normal soap, this is fabric softener, and this is bleach. Only use bleach on whites!" Her mom reached into a basket to pull out a black shirt. "See all these splotches? The bleach made them. On a white shirt it would make it clean. Remember when your dad squirted ketchup all over his white work shirt? Well, here it is now!" Her mom proudly held up the crisp white shirt. Karina was impressed. "It's just like the way our sins stain our lives, Mom, and Jesus in his huge love for us, removes all those stains leaving us pure and holy!" Her mom smiled. "Exactly!"

How has God's mercy changed you?

Attentive

These Jews were better than the Jews in Thessalonica.
They were eager to hear the things Paul and Silas said.
These Jews in Berea studied the Scriptures every day to
find out if these things were true.

ACTS 17:11 ICB

Did you know that there are people who make fake money?
It is called counterfeit money, and there are whole law
enforcement departments dedicated to finding the people
who make it. What is really interesting, though, is the way
they are trained to know the difference between fake money
and real money—they study the real thing. They don't even
bother trying to know all the different kinds of fake money.
Instead, they spend all their time studying real money, so
they know exactly what it looks and feels like. They are
attentive to the details, so when a fake bill comes along,
they know it immediately.

This is very similar to the truth. Be attentive to the Word of
God. If you know the truth well, you will be able to identify
things that aren't of God.

How can you be more attentive to the Word of God?

Beauty

He has made everything beautiful in its time. He has also given people a sense of who he is. But they can't completely understand what God has done from beginning to end.

ECCLESIASTES 3:11 NIRV

In the middle of March, spring is usually on its way. The grass is turning green, the trees are blooming, and there is beauty at every turn! Have you ever wondered why God made our world beautiful? He could have created us in a gray, dull world, with no color or variety. Instead, he delighted in bringing all the unique flavors, colors, textures, and types into creation.

It tells us what kind of God he is; he is creative and beautiful. He's an artist who wants you to delight in the world around you. Take some time to notice the beauty of God's creation, from the big blue skies with puffy white clouds to the tiniest details on blooming flowers. Thank God for the things that you find.

What beauty do you see around you now?

Celebrate

Celebrate with praises the God and Father of our Lord Jesus Christ, who has shown us his extravagant mercy. For his fountain of mercy has given us a new life—we are reborn to experience a living, energetic hope through the resurrection of Jesus Christ from the dead.

1 PETER 1:3 TPT

What is one important thing to have at every birthday celebration? Presents! Giving one another gifts is a popular way to show you care for someone. Jesus has given us the greatest gift—a new life in God. This means that because of what he did on the cross, we are at peace with God, and our sins are wiped clean.

Because he has given us this gift, we too, can give him a gift in return—our praise! We celebrate what Jesus did for us, and we praise him for who he is. He loves to hear us sing, see us dance, and receive our thanks. Spend time today singing praises to God for all the gifts he's given you. Celebrate! He is a good God.

When was the last time you thanked God for his good gifts?

Logic

"The minds of these people have become stubborn. They do not hear with their ears, and they have closed their eyes. Otherwise they might really understand what they see with their eyes and hear with their ears. They might really understand in their minds and come back to me and be healed."

MATTHEW 13:15 NCV

In this verse, Jesus was talking about a group of people called the Pharisees. The Pharisees knew the Scriptures, they had seen Jesus perform miracles, they even knew the prophecies about him; yet they couldn't understand that he was God. It didn't seem logical to them. This is similar to wearing glasses. Before you get your new glasses, you think that the way you see is the way everyone sees. But once you get your glasses and put them on, everything changes. Suddenly you can see clearly. From then on, you want to wear your glasses because you can see so much better.

Many people in the world know about Jesus, but they don't understand the logic that he is God. Pray today for people to know Jesus and to know that he is God.

How clear is Scripture to you? Do you need to wear your spiritual glasses more often?

Same

God is not a man, so he does not lie. He is not human, so he does not change his mind. Has he ever spoken and failed to act? Has he ever promised and not carried it through?

NUMBERS 23:19 NLT

Marlisse glanced at the clock again. She hated Saturday mornings. Ever since her parents had separated, her dad was supposed to pick her up on Saturday mornings at eight o'clock. Each week she waited as she ate a bowl of cereal, and each week he failed to show up. She felt confused and sad. Why didn't he come? She wished she could count on him.

As her cereal milk turned brown from her Cocoa Pebbles, she opened the Bible that Ms. James, her Sunday school teacher, had given her. She was just a few months in on her Bible reading plan, in the book of Numbers. When she came across verse nineteen in chapter twenty-three, she stopped. It moved her heart to read that unlike earthly fathers, God would never lie to her, never fail her, and never make a promise he could not keep. She knew then that no matter what, she could rely on God. He would always be the same.

What are you relying on God for today?

Diligent

The LORD says, "I will save the one who loves me. I will keep
him safe, because he trusts in me. He will call out to me,
and I will answer him. I will be with him in times of trouble.
I will save him and honor him. I will give him a long
and full life. I will save him."

PSALM 91:14-16 NIRV

Has a parent ever said to you, "Why do I have to repeat
myself?" They may be annoyed that they have to say again
what they already said, but repeating a phrase is one way to
make sure people know to listen. It indicates that something
important is being said.

In the Bible, sometimes the same word is said twice in a row
so that the reader pays attention. In the verse above, count
how many times it says, "I will." How many did you get? God
is the "I" in these verses, and he's the one doing all the work!
He has promised to save us, keep us safe, answer us, be with
us in hard times, honor us, and give us long and full lives.
What beautiful promises! Sometimes your mind can be full
of doubts, so choose to trust in the Word of God. Listen to
the track that is on repeat: "I will always love you," says the
God of the universe.

How can you absorb the truth of God's love?

Delight

Enjoy serving the LORD,
and he will give you what you want.

PSALM 37:4 NCV

A janitor walks around with many keys on their key ring. They have keys to the classrooms, the closets, various machines, and many other things. The keys help the janitor get to where he needs to be and do what needs to be done.

God has given us many keys for the very same reason. The difference is his keys are in the form of verses. Our verse above is one of them. The key to being happy is serving and loving the Lord, and therefore it's not found in material things! When we remember this key, it will help us walk through the right doors and find happiness instead of constantly trying to walk through the wrong doors. Happiness is found in Jesus alone. Don't put your hope in getting that new device or toy, or in having lots of things. This will not make you happy. True happiness is found in Jesus alone, and he will provide all that you need.

What is the key to happiness?

Renewed

Do not be shaped by this world. Instead be changed within
by a new way of thinking. Then you will be able to decide
what God wants for you. And you will be able to know what
is good and pleasing to God and what is perfect.

ROMANS 12:2 ICB

It doesn't matter how old you get, playing with play dough
is super fun. There is a wide variety of colors and smells. It
squishes amazingly between your fingers as you are rolling it
onto the table. The best part is probably the many different
things you can make. The possibilities are endless! All you
need is an imagination, and you can shape anything.

We are like play dough. We are either being shaped to look
more like Jesus or like the sinful world around us. If we want
to look like Jesus, we need to let his Word shape us. We need
to throw out the sinful ways of thinking like old, dry play
dough. Instead, we need to memorize Scripture and change
our thinking to be aligned with Christ.

What Bible verse will you memorize this week?

Daring

Some trust in chariots. Some trust in horses.
But we trust in the LORD our God.

PSALM 20:7 NIRV

When most of the world was ruled by kings and queens, it was common to know the strength of an empire by the size of its army. If its army had many horses (because no one had cars) and many chariots (because planes had not been invented), you knew it was a strong, thriving empire. It would make people feel safe if they lived in a strong empire that could crush the other ones around them that were threatening.

It's good to feel safe, but the trust of these citizens was in the army, and that is misplaced. We shouldn't count on our parents, or our older siblings, or any army to keep us safe. We shouldn't put our trust in our own strength or the strength of others. The most powerful, trustworthy one of all, is God, and that is where our trust should be. He can defeat any army, and he has promised to always protect us.

Is it more daring to put your trust in God or in yourself?

Recognized

Don't let anyone think less of you because you are young.
Be an example to all believers in what you say, in the way
you live, in your love, your faith, and your purity.

1 TIMOTHY 4:12 NLT

When we put our faith in Jesus, we receive the Holy Spirit.
He is the one who comforts us, encourages us, helps us learn,
and guides us in life. As a child, you receive the same, whole
Holy Spirit that any adult does. God doesn't send a half-
size portion of the Spirit to you, or a ten-year-old piece of
himself. You are just as equipped as any adult believer.

Don't wait to grow up to become active in your faith. You
can become more like Christ now! You can do all the things
that grown Christians do, like praying for others, using
your gifts, learning the Bible, and so much more! You are
an important part of the body of Christ, and you should
recognize that.

Do you Recognize the Power of God working in you?

Brightness

The Son is the shining brightness of God's glory. He is the exact likeness of God's being. He uses his powerful word to hold all things together. He provided the way for people to be made pure from sin. Then he sat down at the right hand of the King, the Majesty in heaven. So he became higher than the angels. The name he received is more excellent than theirs.

HEBREWS 1:3-4 NIRV

Do you have a favorite movie or TV star? If so, you've probably watched many of their films, but you've probably never met them in real life. The only way you know them is from a distance. It might feel like you know them since you watch things they are in and you read about them, but in reality, you don't know them at all.

It can be the same with Jesus. We can be told about him, see him work in others' lives, and yet still not know him. Don't base your whole faith on what other people tell you about Jesus. Get to know him yourself! He is brighter than anything you can imagine.

How bright is Jesus' Light in your Life?

GLORY

Through our faith, Christ has brought us into that blessing of God's grace that we now enjoy. And we are happy because of the hope we have of sharing God's glory.

ROMANS 5:2 ICB

Imagine you move into a new house, but when you move it is wintertime, so you have no idea what the yard looks like. When spring arrives, you notice some plants coming up in the back corner. Forgetting about them, a few weeks later you catch a glimpse of pink. When you walk out there, you are surrounded by beautiful, big blooms! You now get to enjoy the lovely flowers.

God's glory is evident in the world around us. We don't always plant the seeds or water the plants or tend the soil. We might do no work, yet we get to enjoy all the beautiful benefits of his glory, like faith, grace, and endless blessings.

When have you seen the glory of God?

Deliverance

His light broke through the darkness and
he led us out in freedom from death's dark shadow
and snapped every one of our chains.

PSALM 107:14 TPT

Do you know a really fun word? Spelunking. What does it mean? It is the practice of exploring caves. If you were to go spelunking you would wear a hard hat in case of falling rocks, and you would take a rope, and wear sturdy shoes. Of course, a flashlight would be a necessity. Caves can be incredibly dark.

Darker than the darkest cave is how you could describe the impact of sin and death on our lives. It's impossible for us to find a way out on our own. Yet Jesus chose to go spelunking through the darkness of hell, and in that choice, he delivered us from sin. Did he need a flashlight? No, because he is the Light of the World!

What has Jesus delivered you from recently?

Awesome

Let us be thankful, because we have a kingdom that cannot be shaken. We should worship God in a way that pleases him with respect and fear.

HEBREWS 12:28 NCV

When you think of worshiping God, what comes to your mind? Maybe all you imagine is people singing at church. Did you know that worship can be so much more than the songs you sing? Worshiping God is about a heart that wants to do his will. It is about expressing your love for him. Some people express their love through paintings and drawings. Some do it through poetry or songs. Others love God through their acts of service, or by taking a hike and enjoying the beauty of nature.

Worship is when our heart's desire is to thank God. If we search, there are many ways to express that gratefulness. You don't have to wait for Sunday morning to worship the awesome God. There are many ways you can express your love for him.

How can you worship God for his awesomeness today?

Authentic

My goal while I was with you was to talk about only one thing. And that was Jesus Christ and his death on the cross. When I came to you, I was weak and very afraid and trembling all over.

1 CORINTHIANS 2:2-3 NIRV

When you read about the people in the Bible, do you ever think of them as superheroes? Take the apostle Paul, for instance. He was a really bad guy until Jesus got a hold of his life. Then he ended up preaching to a ton of people and writing a lot of the New Testament!

The people you read about in the Bible are humans just like you. They dealt with fear, and they made mistakes. They were real. They were authentic. There is nothing that made them superheroes, but when they chose to let the Holy Spirit work through them, they became powerful. Paul was afraid when he went to tell the people in the church at Corinth about Jesus. Despite this fear, he obeyed God, and great things happened.

How do you feel knowing the heroes in the Bible were humans just like you?

Capable

"You have a large number of skilled stonemasons and carpenters and craftsmen of every kind. You have expert goldsmiths and silversmiths and workers of bronze and iron. Now begin the work, and may the LORD be with you!"

1 CHRONICLES 22:15-16 NLT

Morelle watched the band set up as her mom worked on the sound board. It was Sunday morning again, and although she loved listening to the worship team practice, she badly wanted to join them. Finally, she got up the courage to tell her mom. Her mom pointed across the room to Jake, the worship leader, and told her to speak to him. She gingerly approached him and said she wanted to sing with them. "Of course!" Jake said and told her what song to practice. He knew she was capable of learning and doing a good job.

All week Morelle practiced her song, and then Sunday morning she took the stage and sang with the team. Afterward, her mom gave her a hug and told her how proud she was that she was using her gift of music to serve the Lord. Morelle had never thought of it that way. She was thankful that Jesus had given her the capability to sing.

How can you use your gift to serve the Lord?

Extra

Every gift God freely gives us is good and perfect,
streaming down from the Father of lights,
who shines from the heavens with no hidden shadow
or darkness and is never subject to change.

JAMES 1:17 TPT

Not all gifts come wrapped in beautiful packages with a shiny bow. God has given you many gifts; can you spot them? You woke up this morning. Another day has been given to you. That is an amazing gift! You have friends and family, and even though some days it might not seem like a gift, life would be lonely without them. The fact that you are able to read this book is a huge gift. What did you eat today? Do you have toys and a warm bed?

Isn't it interesting when we start to look around, how many gifts begin to pop out? There is so much to be thankful for. You've also been given the gift of the Holy Spirit, to guide and comfort you. You are blessed with so much extra, there isn't enough wrapping paper in the world to contain it.

What extra blessings can you thank God for today?

APRIL

The LORD gives me strength

and protects me.

He has saved me.

He is my God, I will praise him.

He is my father's God,

and I will honor him.

EXODUS 15:2 NIRV

Aware

Keep me from looking at worthless things.
Let me live by your word.

PSALM 119:37 NCV

The older you get the more choices you will make regarding the ways you spend your time. Obviously, you have school that takes up a large chunk of your day and sleeping covers most of the night. What do you do with the hours in between? With the freedom of choice comes the pitfalls of using your time for things that are worthless.

You could spend every one of those hours mindlessly playing video games, scrolling social media, or watching TV. Or you could be aware of how those things, though not necessarily bad, can be a waste of your time.

After you spend hours on social media, do you feel Refreshed or gross?

FoLLow

Jesus said to his disciples, "If any of you wants to be
my follower, you must give up your own way,
take up your cross, and follow me."

MATTHEW 16:24 NLT

In the days of Jesus, there were many teachers called rabbis.
The rabbis would teach people about God and the Old
Testament. The people who followed them were devoted
to learning whatever they could about God, so they would
follow their rabbis around. They would listen and ask
questions. In fact, they followed them so much on the dry,
dusty roads, that there was a saying: "May you be covered
in the dust of your rabbi." This meant that you would be
following your teacher so closely that you were covered in
the dust that he kicked up as he walked.

Jesus is our rabbi. We should be covered in his dust from
following him closely, listening to his Word, and obeying him.

How cLoseLy do you foLLow Jesus?

Adoption

You have not received a spirit that makes you fearful slaves. Instead, you received God's Spirit when he adopted you as his own children.

ROMANS 8:15 NLT

You might be wondering why you need to be adopted if you already have parents. Every person needs to be spiritually adopted by God. We are separated from him because of sin, and without adoption we are without a home. God's plan was to make us his own children, so we can have a safe home.

You have a Father who looks out for you. Being God's child makes you very special. Sometimes you might think negative things like you are not wanted or loved. When you feel like this, remember what God says about you. You are chosen and adopted, and you're a very special member of his family.

How does it feel to know you are adopted by God?

Abundant

They eat well because there is
more than enough in your house.
You let them drink from your river
that flows with good things.

PSALM 36:8 NIRV

There was a long line at the ice cream stand. It was opening day, and the line stretched down the street. Waiting impatiently, Arielle watched as person after person left with their favorite flavors. I hope they don't run out of mine! she thought anxiously. She noticed the ice cream levels were looking really low. Just as she was about to freak out, a woman walked up to the freezer with a whole cart of new buckets. She saw Arielle's anxious stare and met it with a smile. "Don't worry, kiddo," she laughed. "There is more than enough! I have a storehouse full, and you will get your share and then some!"

We often act like Arielle, worrying that there won't be enough of whatever we need, but God has a storehouse full of everything: mercy, forgiveness, healing, and much more. God can abundantly provide for it all.

What do you want God to provide for you today?

Pleasing

"I hope I continue to please you, sir," she replied.
"You have comforted me by speaking so kindly to me,
even though I am not one of your workers."

RUTH 2:13 NLT

If you want to read a story about a brave woman who followed God, look no further than the book of Ruth in the Old Testament. Ruth was alive during a hard time in Israel's history. It was a time when people did whatever they wanted, and they didn't listen to God. Ruth had a hard life. Shortly after she was married her father-in-law died, and then her young husband did as well. She, however, loved her mother-in-law, Naomi.

Ruth and Naomi had to travel back to Naomi's homeland in order to survive once their husbands had died. When they arrived, Ruth went to find work and to beg in order to get food for Naomi and herself. She met a man named Boaz who loved God and lived by his ways. He showed kindness to Ruth, and eventually they got married. Ruth was the great-grandmother of King David and in the lineage of Jesus himself!

How can you be pleasing to God?

COMPLETION

God began doing a good work in you. And he will continue
it until it is finished when Jesus Christ comes again.
I am sure of that.

PHILIPPIANS 1:6 ICB

Have you ever had the chance to make something out of
clay? It can be really fun to shape and pull the clay and
to mold it in your hands in the hopes of making it into
something beautiful. Maybe you have seen coffee mugs or
vases made by potters, and you wanted to try to make your
own. It's not as easy as it looks!

What if, in the middle of shaping a coffee mug, you just gave
up? Could you use that lump of clay to drink out of? Of
course not! The clay needs to go through the whole proper
process in order to be a good mug. It must be molded, fired,
glazed, and all the other steps involved in the making of a
good, beautiful, and sturdy coffee mug. In the same way,
God is not going to stop working in your life. He will make
sure that all the good things he has planned for you get
completed. What a beautiful promise!

What can you feel God working on in your life?

Right

"I, Nebuchadnezzar, give praise and honor and glory to the King of heaven. Everything he does is right and fair, and he is able to make proud people humble."

DANIEL 4:37 NCV

Reputation is a big word that means the character you are known for, whether true or untrue. For instance, if you have a reputation of being stinky, that means you've probably been stinky often, or people have said to others that you are. That example is a silly one, but reputations are important.

Did you know God has a reputation as well? Many people will say different things about God, but what is most important is what the Bible says about God. The Bible tells us how God truly is. In our verse today, the Bible is telling us that God is right and fair.

Isn't it comforting to know that the God we serve is always Right?

Effective

The prayer of a Godly person is powerful.

JAMES 5:16 NIRV

When you pray, does it ever feel like you are just talking to the wind? The fact that we cannot see God face-to-face can be discouraging for our prayer life. It's far easier to speak to someone and relate to them when you can see their face and watch their expressions. Sometimes we have to exercise our muscles of faith by just trusting what the Bible says.

The Bible tells us that our prayers are powerful, and they matter. We are assured that they work, and God hears them all. This is the truth we must remember when doubt comes into our mind. Praying helps us build a relationship with God and get to know his heart better. It's a wonderful adventure full of good things, so don't give up! Keep praying.

HOW CAN YOU MAKE YOUR PRAYERS MORE effective?

Acceptable

Abraham was, humanly speaking, the founder of our Jewish nation. What did he discover about being made right with God? If his good deeds had made him acceptable to God, he would have had something to boast about. But that was not God's way. For the Scriptures tell us, "Abraham believed God, and God counted him as righteous because of his faith."

ROMANS 4:1-3 NIV

The normal flow of our world seems to be that if you work hard for something, you get it. In the area of being forgiven for our sins, that is not the case. You cannot ever do enough good in your life to get yourself into heaven. No matter how hard you try, that's not how it works—and thankfully so!

The only way to be in heaven later is through God's grace through his Son, Jesus Christ. That means if we have faith in God and Christ's sacrifice on the cross, which made us acceptable to him, that is all that matters. Trusting God to do what he says and that his Word is true is the most difficult part of understanding, but it is the most important thing of all. So, if you ever find yourself constantly working harder to get God to approve of you, you don't need to!

Do you know you are accepted by God just as you are?

Convinced

I am absolutely sure that not even death or life can separate us from God's love. Not even angels or demons, the present or the future, or any powers can separate us. Not even the highest places or the lowest, or anything else in all creation can separate us. Nothing at all can ever separate us from God's love. That's because of what Christ Jesus our Lord has done.

ROMANS 8:38-39 NIRV

Did you know there are places in the world where it gets so cold you can throw boiling hot water into the air, and it will immediately turn into snow? In these places, it's so cold that it's common for doors to freeze shut. You have to be careful when you go outside because if you place your skin against anything metal, it can stick to it! It is then really difficult to get unstuck!

When you think of God's inseparable love for you, maybe this can serve as a tangible reminder. The love of God is millions of times stronger than the most frozen door. That's how much he loves you! Nothing can separate you from him. What an amazing promise! The next time you are feeling distant from God, remember his promise to stick close by you, to never leave you.

How close do you feel to God?

Rational

Stay away from anger and revenge.
Keep envy far from you, for it only leads you into lies.

PSALM 37:8 TPT

Have you ever gotten a new toy with an instruction manual, and then felt confused about how to put it together? Why can't they just make the instructions clear and simple? Sometimes we feel that way about the Bible too. What is it the author is trying to tell us to do in this Scripture? Stay away from anger, revenge, and envy!

Although it's easy to say, it's hard to do. Maybe you see a classmate who always has a better lunch than you, and it makes you envious. Or perhaps you have a sibling who always seems to get away with things, and that makes you angry. These temptations are difficult, but there is another way to respond to your frustrations. Ask God to help you have the strength to do what is right, and to turn from evil.

How can you keep your heart from turning toward envy?

Rich

You are rich in everything—in faith, in speaking, in knowledge, in truly wanting to help, and in the love you learned from us. In the same way, be strong also in the grace of giving.

2 CORINTHIANS 8:7 NCV

Much like the church in Corinth, you have been richly blessed by God. If you are reading this right now, you have the ability to read, which is something many people do not have. If you go to school, you are given a chance that around a hundred and twenty-nine million girls in the world are not given. Do you have your own room? Are you provided with hot meals every day? Is there a roof over your head? The blessings go on and on.

Let's thank God for the many things he has given us. Let's be on the lookout for ways we can give to others. At first, giving may be hard, but the more you do it, the easier it becomes. There is so much joy to be found in spreading the blessings of God. Try it! Share your lunch, pay attention to someone who is often ignored, or help a friend with their homework. Ask God to show you how to be generous today.

What could you give to someone today?

IMPORTANT

"If you tenderly care for this little child on my behalf,
you are tenderly caring for me. And if you care for me,
you are honoring my Father who sent me.
For the one who is least important in your eyes
is actually the most important one of all."

LUKE 9:48 TPT

Has anyone ever made you feel like you are not important just because you are a child? It can be so hurtful when careless words or actions sting our hearts. People like that are not honoring the way of Jesus because Jesus loved children. He requested the adults make a way for kids to come to him because he wanted to teach them and bless them. He spoke about kids often in his teaching, even telling adults that they need to become child-like in their faith.

You are not less of a Christian because you are young. The same Holy Spirit that lives inside every adult believer lives inside of you. That is powerful! Don't take to heart the hurtful words that some have said. Instead, cling to the truth that Jesus loves all the children.

How important do you think you are to Jesus?

Servant

"The greatest among you must be a servant."

MATTHEW 23:11 NLT

"A servant?" Jessica exclaimed in disgust. When she thought of a servant, she pictured an old woman with a bent back and a feather duster in hand. A servant runs around doing all the hard work. She sweeps, cooks, cleans, fetches things, and makes her snooty master lemonade on hot days. "No thanks!" she thought.

Is this what Jesus meant when we said that we should be like servants? Not exactly. A servant is a person who performs different services for other people. Doctors serve their patients with medical care. Teachers serve their students by training and educating them. It is the actions of one person to benefit another that make them a servant. Jesus was the ultimate example of a servant by going as far as dying on the cross for us. Being a servant shows humility and obedience. It doesn't always mean just cleaning the house, but it does mean putting others' needs first.

Can you show the love of Christ by serving someone today?

Saved

The message of the cross seems foolish to those who are lost and dying. But it is God's power to us who are being saved.

1 CORINTHIANS 1:18 NIRV

If you learn nothing else in your life, make sure you learn this—Jesus is God. When mankind through Adam chose to disobey God, and he pridefully did exactly what God said not to do, sin entered the whole earth. Each of us sin, and not one is perfect. God, however, is perfect and holy. In order for us to be with God, we too must be made perfect. How can this happen? A sacrifice needed to be made.

God had a plan—the plan of the cross. Jesus came to earth as a man, lived a sinless life, and then was put to death on the cross for our sins. By doing this, he broke the power of sin and death that was over us, and he set us free. In order to accept this freedom, all we have to do is believe that Jesus did this, that he is God, and repent of our sins. To repent means to admit we have done wrong, turn from the bad things we do, and choose to do things God's way instead. Then we walk in the freedom, power, and complete love of God.

What does it mean to you to be saved?

Satisfied

"I am the Bread of Life. Come every day to me and you will never be hungry. Believe in me and you will never be thirsty."

JOHN 6:35 TPT

Yum, breakfast! It's the most important meal of the day. What is your favorite breakfast food? Is it pancakes dripping in maple syrup, waffles with whip cream, cheesy scrambled eggs and bacon, or granola and yogurt? The list goes on, and you are probably getting hungry just reading this!

Just as people say that breakfast is the most important meal of the day, the time you spend with Jesus is the most important time of your day in order to feed your soul. The time you spend reading your Bible and praying in the mornings is like having a big, filling breakfast for your soul. The Holy Spirit refreshes your spirit, teaches you new things, hands out new mercies, and equips you for the day to come. Just like skipping breakfast can leave you feeling weak and hangry, missing your time in the Word will leave your soul starving.

How satisfied is your soul?

Redemption

At one time you were separated from God. You were his enemies in your minds, and the evil things you did were against God. But now God has made you his friends again. He did this through Christ's death in the body so that he might bring you into God's presence as people who are holy, with no wrong, and with nothing of which God can judge you guilty.

COLOSSIANS 1:21-22 NCV

"What is the gospel?" Samantha had heard that word many times at church but didn't know what it meant. Ms. Brown smiled at her. She loved it when the kids asked such great questions. "Gospel means 'good news.' It is a word we use to refer to how Jesus has saved us." She opened her Bible to the book of Colossians and read the Scripture above. "This verse explains it well; we were God's enemies, and we had chosen to be that. But God wanted us to be his friends, so he made a way for us to have peace with him again. Through Jesus, we are made holy, and we become friends with God."

Samantha felt excited and happy. What Ms. Brown had just shown her was good news for sure! She couldn't wait to share this good news with her friends at school.

What does Redemption mean to you?

Choices

My brothers and sisters, you were chosen to be free.
But don't use your freedom as an excuse to live under
the power of sin. Instead, serve one another in love.

GALATIANS 5:13 NIRV

The older you get, the more choices you get to make on your own. This can be a pretty exciting thing about getting older! You get to choose what you want to eat, what you wear, what shows you watch, what activities interest you most. But with the fun choices also comes harder choices.

Every day you will be faced with choices that have to do with the kingdom of God: will I follow what my sin nature tells me to do, or will I do things in obedience to God? When faced with the decision to tell a lie or not, which will you choose? When faced with the choice to hit your sibling or not, will you choose God's way or your own? Choices can be fun, but they can also be hard. Ask God to give you the strength to choose what is right today.

What good choices can you make this week?

TRUST

When I am afraid,
I will trust you.
I praise God for his word.
I trust God. So I am not afraid.
What can human beings do to me?

PSALM 56:3-4 ICB

Boom! Crash! The loud noises caused Kara to dive once again under the covers even though they failed to fully hide the bright flash of light that followed. Kara was ten years old, and she still hated thunderstorms. Her siblings made her feel silly for her fear, but she just couldn't seem to make it go away. In order to get to her parents' room, she would have to go right past her siblings' rooms, and that was only if she could get the courage to get out of bed! As another crash of thunder rumbled in her ears, she prayed that Jesus would let her know how near he is, just like her mom had taught her.

Suddenly, she remembered Psalms 56, the psalm that her teacher was having them memorize this year. She whispered it to herself. "I trust God, so I am not afraid." It made her feel better to know that no matter how big her fear may seem, God was bigger, he was nearby, and she could always trust him.

Do you trust God in the scary moments?

Unshakable

Stand strong. Do not let anything move you. Always give yourselves fully to the work of the Lord, because you know that your work in the Lord is never wasted.

1 CORINTHIANS 15:58 NCV

In the lake or the oceans, buoys are used to mark the position of an underwater danger or as a mooring spot instead of having to use an anchor. If you've ever seen buoys bobbing off the coast, they move back and forth and all around as the water hits them. They do, however, stay within a short range of one spot. How is that possible? Well, the buoys are held in place by a strong anchor which goes down to the bottom of the water. No matter what strong wind and waves come, the buoy will stay in place.

We can stay steady in our faith if our hearts are anchored deeply in Christ. If he is what we are holding onto since he is holding onto us, no storms in life will ever knock us off course.

What Makes you feel unshakable?

Good

Taste and see that the LORD is good.
Blessed is the person who goes to him for safety.

PSALM 34:8 NIRV

What is your favorite meal in the whole world? Think about what food you love and just how wonderful it tastes. You look forward to eating it. You often ask your parents to make it. You think about eating it every day for the rest of your life and never get tired of it. This food that you are imagining—how do you know it is good? You know it is good because you have experienced it! It's not because you have seen it in a magazine and then think it might be good; it's because you have eaten it and tasted it.

In the same way, when we experience the love of God, it's like tasting his goodness. When we notice him moving in our lives, we can see his goodness. Like that wonderful food that we have tasted, you can't just hear about God or just read about him; you have to experience him for yourself. Ask God to let you taste and see his goodness today.

Do you see the goodness of God in your life?

Unashamed

Make every effort to give yourself to God as the kind of person he will approve. Be a worker who is not ashamed and who uses the true teaching in the right way.

2 TIMOTHY 2:15 NCV

Lily wanted to invite her friend, Tara, to come to church with her. Lily loved her church and the kind people who attended there. She learned so much every week about God and enjoyed how her teacher, Ms. Brown, taught her from the Bible. Tara didn't go to church, but they had been friends since she moved to Lily's town. Lily was nervous to invite Tara though. What if Tara made fun of her? What if she said no?

Lily was facing a problem common to what we all face. Do we not tell others about Jesus, or invite them to church, or share the Bible with them because of what they might say or think? What if they reject us or make fun of us? This is a real fear, but God can give us the courage to speak up. He wants us to share the good news with all those around us. No matter how others treat us, he will never leave us or reject us.

Is there someone you can tell about Jesus this week?

Teachable

"I tell you the truth, unless you turn from your sins
and become like little children, you will never
get into the Kingdom of Heaven."

MATTHEW 18:3 NLT

When you read this verse, you may be wondering how it
can apply to you. After all, you are already a child! As far as
you know, adults can't become kids again, so what on earth
did Jesus mean by this? Though you may have a deep desire
to grow up, there are many wonderful things about being a
kid, and Jesus knew that. One of those wonderful things is
the way children trust completely. Kids trust their parents to
take care of them and they love them.

Even when earthly parents fail, God never will. We can trust
in him to always love us, care for us, provide for us, and be
there when we need him. Kids are known for asking a lot of
questions. For the sake of your faith, that's not a bad thing
at all! Jesus welcomes all the questions as another way you
can get to know him. Listening to his answers makes you a
teachable person.

How can you learn from Jesus?

Prayerful

Always be joyful. Pray continually, and give thanks whatever happens. That is what God wants for you in Christ Jesus.

1 THESSALONIANS 5:16-18 NCV

What do you think it means to pray continually? To do something continually means to do something repeatedly all the time. Is God asking us to do nothing else but pray? Well, not exactly. What is meant here is that anytime and anywhere you happen to be, you can pray to God. You don't have to be in a church building or somewhere special.

There are other things that some of us do repeatedly, like worrying. You can replace your worrying with praying. When something worries you, instead of dwelling on it, pray to God about it! Tell him what worries you. When something fills you with joy, thank God for it! Share your joy with him. Praying continually simply means that God is in our thoughts through your whole day.

How do you feel knowing that God always wants to hear from you?

HARMONY

Make allowance for each other's faults, and forgive anyone
who offends you. Remember, the Lord forgave you,
so you must forgive others.

COLOSSIANS 3:13 NLT

Grace lowered her head in shame. Her mom had found the
book and journal set that she had stolen from the store. Not
only had she stolen it, but she lied to her mom when she
was asked about it. Surprisingly, Grace's mom gently lifted
the edge of her chin, and said she forgave her. Her mom's
forgiveness felt like a weight lifted off her chest. As Grace
skipped out to go to her room, she glanced inside to see her
sister messing with her things. Grace felt angry. How many
times did she need to tell her sister not to touch her stuff!

Grace huffed into the room, and when her sister saw her, she
asked for forgiveness. No way! Grace thought. This is the last
straw. Grace's mom came into the room right behind her,
and Grace remembered how just minutes earlier, her mom
had forgiven her for a really big thing. She understood then
that she should forgive her sister for this much smaller thing.
God has forgiven every single one of your sins. Likewise,
when others sin against us, we need to truly forgive them.

How can you live in harmony with the people around you?

Promises

The Lord is not slow in doing what he promised—the way
some people understand slowness. But God is being patient
with you. He does not want anyone to be lost. He wants
everyone to change his heart and life.

2 PETER 3:9 ICB

When you see the news on TV or overhear people talking,
you might hear about a lot of bad things happening in our
world. Maybe in your own life you've had a taste of this.
Have you ever wondered why, if bad things keep happening,
Jesus doesn't just come back and make it all stop?

This verse for today gives us part of the answer. Jesus loves
each and every person on earth so much that he wants to
make sure that every person has the opportunity to know
him. He is patient, giving them time to seek and find
him. He wants every person to live forever with him in
heaven. That can be hard when people keep sinning and
hurting themselves and one another, but Jesus is also a kind
gentleman, and he is not willing to force any of us into loving
him. He patiently waits for us to choose him.

What Promise are you Most waiting to see God fulfill?

Holy

God has chosen you and made you his holy people. He loves you. So you should always clothe yourselves with mercy, kindness, humility, gentleness, and patience.

COLOSSIANS 3:12 NCV

After a long day of playing outside in the warm spring rain, your parents probably ask you to take a shower before bed. That way, you are fresh and clean from the splatters and mud before you put on your clean pajamas.

To be holy means that your spirit has been set apart and made clean. This is not done by anything you can do, but by believing in what Jesus did on the cross. When God makes us clean, we then can choose to "clothe" our spirits in the clean outfits of characteristics like kindness and patience. Choosing other clothes, like being unkind, impatient, not showing mercy to others, or being brutal, would be like showering and then putting on gross, stained, dirty pajamas. Ew! Remember the clean pajamas. Remember you have been made clean, and therefore put on daily the clean clothes for your spirit.

How does it feel to be clean?

Bound

Over all these good things put on love.
Love holds them all together perfectly
as if they were one.

COLOSSIANS 3:14 NIRV

Sally was running up the basement stairs, through the living room, straight around the corner into the dining room, and through the doorway when—BAM! She ran smack into her little brother. Unfortunately, he just so happened to be carrying his prized Lego creation he was taking to enter into the county fair. CRASH! All the pieces scattered on the tile floor. Both Sally and her brother's face sank into looks of despair.

After a million "I'm sorries," her brother calmed down enough to listen to their father who had offered to help. "Sometimes people who build Legos for competition bind them together with superglue. That way, they won't ever break apart." This reminded Sally of the verse she had read last week. Love is like the superglue of our lives, holding all the pieces together and making them into a masterpiece.

Who can you choose to love better this week?

HONOR

Be devoted to tenderly loving your fellow believers as
members of one family. Try to outdo yourselves
in respect and honor of one another.

ROMANS 12:10 TPT

Do you enjoy a little competition? Here is one you may have
never done before. Try to see if you can be MORE respectful
of those around you than you have been in the past. For
instance, when your parents ask you to do a chore or to get
ready for school, don't complain. Just do it! When you are
at school and everyone is making fun of that one girl again,
walk over to her and be kind! Simple actions like these are
how you can show love, respect, and honor to people you
are around daily. When you are choosing popsicles, let your
sibling choose first.

Jesus was known as the servant to all. That doesn't mean he
acted like a slave, but it does means he was loving, honoring,
and respectful to the people with whom he spoke. We can
mold our lives to be like him when we do the same.

How could you show honor to someone today?

Represent

Whatever you do or say, do it as a representative of the Lord Jesus, giving thanks through him to God the Father.

COLOSSIANS 3:17 NLT

Does your school have a school spirit day? That is a special day, set aside to have a fun time with everyone dressing in the school colors. Someone even comes as the school mascot. If your school doesn't do this, think of a professional sports team, and notice how many of the fans wear their team's colors and paint their faces in those colors. This way everyone knows which team they support!

In the same way, as a Christian, our words and actions are like face paint and team colors for Jesus. You can easily tell other people how great God is by simply giving thanks to him for the good things in your life. Instead of saying, "That was lucky," say, "God did that." Or when you have a God-story of him doing something in your life like healing you or helping you, don't forget to give him credit. That way you can show how great God is to everyone everywhere!

How can you represent God this week?

MAY

"Here is what I am commanding you to do. Be strong and brave. Do not be afraid. Do not lose hope. I am the LORD your God. I will be with you everywhere you go."

JOSHUA 1:9 NIRV

Friendly

Accept each other just as Christ has accepted you
so that God will be given glory.

ROMANS 15:7 NLT

Maddie loved her new gymnastics class. Although she had
joined as an eight-year-old, she was quickly catching up to
the skill level of the other girls who had been flipping and
back-springing together since they were six. One day the
coach said class was over. Instead of all the girls running
to the locker room together like normal, they all ran to the
party room. It was Willow's birthday! Willow had invited the
whole class except for Maddie.

There are many reasons why Willow may not have invited
Maddie, but that doesn't make the pain of being left out any
less. Few things hurt as badly as being left out and feeling
alone. With this in mind, who can you invite to be included
today?

How can you make someone feel accepted?

Adore

How right they are to adore you.

SONG OF SOLOMON 1:4 NLT

If you love princess stories, Song of Solomon is the book of the Bible for you. You can also check out the book of Esther to read about a fierce princess who risked her life to do what God asked of her. Esther ended up saving her people. Song of Solomon is a love story that takes place right before the wedding of the two people in the book. Though there is no evil witch or poisoned apple in this tale, it is one that speaks to us of a deep love.

There is a really cool thing about this. The church—which is all the people who believe in Jesus—is the bride, and Jesus is the groom. It's a way of talking about his love for us. You can say to Jesus how much you adore him, and there are so many reasons to love him!

What do you adore about Jesus?

Appreciate

I praise you because you remember me in everything, and you follow closely the teachings just as I gave them to you.

1 CORINTHIANS 11:2 NCV

When school is almost out for the year, some people count down the days, make one of those countdown paper chains, or eagerly mark days off on a calendar. Before you toss your notebooks and pens into the wind, why not take some time to think about someone who doesn't hear a lot of praise—your teacher! They work hard daily to help you grow and learn.

Sunday school teachers, youth pastors, and senior pastors also do the same to help you grow in God's Word. God has blessed you with many people in your life who teach you in order to help you grow. Take some time today to make a card, or even just go up to that teacher and tell them thank you for all that they do. Your appreciation of their hard work can be so encouraging to them!

Which teacher can you thank this week?

Bold

The thing I want and hope for is that I will not fail Christ in
anything. I hope that I will have the courage now, as always,
to show the greatness of Christ in my life here on earth.
I want to do that if I die or if I live.

PHILIPPIANS 1:20 ICB

Believing in Jesus is not the norm. In fact, most people don't
believe in him. Living according to the Bible goes against the
way many people live. Choices like treating others the way
you would like to be treated, loving your enemy as yourself,
granting forgiveness and mercy to all—these are things Jesus
did, and he wants us to do, but the world doesn't necessarily
do them.

It takes courage to be a Christian! We don't have to make up
that courage all on our own. Whenever you ask for it, Jesus
will give you boldness to face your day. When you are unsure
of what to do, Jesus is there to help. Pray to him, tell him
you're afraid, and ask him to fill you with the courage to live
boldly for him!

What do you need boldness for right now?

COMMUNITY

"Where two or three gather together as my followers,
I am there among them."

MATTHEW 18:20 NLT

As a follower of Jesus, you are not expected to everything alone. In fact, he wants just the opposite! Jesus wants you to gather with others who believe in him. At church, we hear strong teaching about God's Word, we meet other people who love Jesus, and we encourage each other with what we have learned about God that week. At church, you can pray for others and be prayed for.

Don't get it mixed up: the church is not a building; it's a group of people. Anywhere a few believers are, the Holy Spirit is present, and the church is gathered. Cool, huh? Maybe this week you and a few friends can get together and pray or study the Bible. Remember that the Holy Spirit is with you in this!

Where is your community of believers?

Shine

Then you will be pure and without blame. Then You will be children of God without fault among sinful and evil people. Then you will shine among them like stars in the sky.

PHILIPPIANS 2:15 NIRV

When you stare up into the night sky on a clear night, it's the stars that first catch your attention. They look like tiny pin pricks in the vast blackness. So many of us are drawn to the light and beauty that stars offer. Look at this verse and count how many times you see the word then. How many did you see? Three times Paul writes it in this verse to the church in Philippi. This indicates that something comes before this verse.

Grab your Bible and look up verse fourteen. What is it talking about? Not grumbling and complaining! How can we become like the stars in the darkness of the world around us? By being thankful. If we are not grumbling, not whining, and not complaining, God will make us shine bright like the stars! Others will be curious about what makes you stand out so much.

How can you shine for Jesus?

Refreshing

The generous will prosper;
those who refresh others will themselves be refreshed.

PROVERBS 11:25 NLT

It's a hot, steamy day. The public pools and splash pads aren't open yet, but you are so excited because your neighbor has a pool and has invited you to come swim! Ms. Lewis is old enough to be your grandma, but she is so generous to share her pool with all the neighborhood kids. In more ways than one, Ms. Lewis has been a refreshing presence in your life.

Ms. Lewis could easily keep her pool all to herself, but because of the love of Jesus in her heart, she chooses to share and be generous with others. God has blessed each of us with unique ways to share. When we do, it's like a refreshing dip in a pool on a scorching day.

How can you be Refreshing to others?

Able

I can do everything through Christ,
who gives me strength.

PHILIPPIANS 4:13 NLT

"Everything?!" Jenny exclaimed to her dad as they biked along the path. Does it really mean everything? She let her imagination roam, thinking about being able to fly or be invisible. Maybe this verse meant she would be super strong, able to lift cars and horses and such. When she told her father her ideas, he lovingly giggled.

Then, he explained the verse. "What it means, Jenny, is that through Christ, you have the power to be content no matter what's happening in the world around you. Paul was in prison when he wrote this. But that didn't matter because he had learned that through Christ, he could find joy no matter where he was." Jenny thought about what her dad said and thought about all the times she needed that kind of strength. It seemed even better than being able to fly.

What do you Need strength foR Right Now?

Rest

"I myself will go with you.
And I will give you victory."

Exodus 33:14 ICB

The Bible, especially the Old Testament, tells a lot of great stories. Some of them are inspiring like David and Goliath, and some can be scary or confusing. Are we supposed to be like the people we read about? The point of these stories is not for us to become like the people, but to become like God. It's to teach us about God's character, and who he is.

When you read a story about a battle or a siege in the book of Exodus, that doesn't mean you need to go off to war. What it does mean is that God is with you no matter where you go. There is a spiritual battle that all Christians are in, and Satan is trying to convince us that God is not good. But he is fighting for us, and we can rest in his promises. When you read the Bible, look for who God is in the story. That's the point!

How can you Rest in God's PRomises?

Glad

We laughed and laughed and overflowed with gladness.
We were left shouting for joy and singing your praise.

PSALM 126:2 TPT

Don't you love those deep belly laughs? It's so fun when you
are rolling on the ground with laughter, unable to stop. It's
amazing when joy and happiness fills your heart so much
you think it might burst!

Do any of these feelings make you think of God, or do you
think God is too serious? Sometimes we get the impression
from some people or from certain churches that God is
always very serious and straight-faced. The truth is, God
loves to laugh. God loves to sing, and he loves joy. He
particularly loves it when we express these wonderful
feelings! So, sing, laugh, dance, and shout. Our God is a
wonderful God!

What are you glad about today?

Consistent

"I will also bless the foreigners
who commit themselves to the Lord,
who serve him and love his name."

ISAIAH 56:6 NLT

In the Bible, you will read a ton about a group of people called the Israelites. You can read about how they started as a family and became a great nation, and how God saved them from slavery in Egypt, and how their family line played a big part all the way up through ancient history.

This group of people was chosen by God to be a blessing to all the other nations on earth. Their job was to show everyone else what life can be like when you choose to serve and love God. They often didn't get it right and you can read all about that in Scripture, but their example shows us that if we choose to follow God, our lives can show others around us how good God is.

How is God consistent to you?

Decent

"Love your enemies! Do good to them. Lend to them without expecting to be repaid. Then your reward from heaven will be very great, and you will truly be acting as children of the Most High, for he is kind to those who are unthankful and wicked."

LUKE 6:35 NLT

When someone is mean to you, what is your first instinct? It's probably to get back at them! That is our sinful nature, and the way we are all born. When we are treated badly, we want to do the same. If we get punched, we want to punch back. If someone embarrasses us, we want to make them feel worse.

Jesus teaches a better way: when people are mean to us, we choose to be kind to them. This is incredibly hard. It goes against everything we want to do. This is how the Holy Spirit works though. When we show the kindness of God to those who hurt us, God can move powerfully through us. The next time you feel tempted to handle a situation your way, ask God to help you respond in kindness.

What does it look like to be decent to people who are unkind?

Energy

Christ is the one we preach about. With all the wisdom we have, we warn and teach everyone. When we bring them to God, we want them to be like Christ. We want them to be grown up as people who belong to Christ. That's what I'm working for. I work hard with all the strength of Christ. His strength works powerfully in me.

COLOSSIANS 1:28-29 NIRV

Paul, a follower of Jesus, was a man on a mission. He was the one who wrote this letter. His goal was to use his life to teach other people about Jesus and to help them know God. Imagine you met a kind, powerful, loving king who promised to give you his whole kingdom. Then he gave you a job to do: tell other people that there is plenty to go around, and everyone can know him and have a share in his kingdom!

This was the mission Paul was on. It's also the mission that God has given us to do. It is God who changes people's hearts, but it is our job to shout the good news from every rooftop. Jesus, our kind King, wants us to know him!

How Much energy do you Put into telLing PeopLe about God?

Determined

When people are tempted and still continue strong, they should be happy. After they have proved their faith, God will reward them with life forever. God promised this to all those who love him.

JAMES 1:12 NCV

Jessica knew it was wrong, but she just couldn't stop thinking about it. She wanted that beautiful olive-green tank top with the matching gold necklace that she saw at the store so badly. Since her mom worked at the store, she had to see the set every time they picked her mom up from work. It was torture! She also knew how easy it would be to just take the shirt and necklace. Her friend Emily had done it before.

Jessica was facing some strong temptation! To be tempted is to feel the pull to do something you know is wrong. It can be like a big game of tug-of-war between what you want and what you know is right. Thankfully, you don't have to pull alone. God is on your team, with all his amazing strength, to help you resist that temptation and win.

How can you determine to overcome temptation?

Equipped

I do live in the world. But I don't fight my battles the way the
people of the world do. The weapons I fight with are not the
weapons the world uses. In fact, it is just the opposite.
My weapons have the power of God to destroy
the camps of the enemy.

2 CORINTHIANS 10:3-4 NIRV

When the Bible speaks about your enemy, who are they
talking about? It's not any person who may have just popped
into your mind. Satan is the real enemy in the Bible who
wants to steal from us and destroy us. He is the one who
doesn't want you to follow Jesus, or to know how much God
loves you. This is your true enemy, more than any bully on
the playground.

How do we fight this enemy? The Word of God is like our
sword, so it's important to read as much of it as we can! It
also helps to memorize it so when we face difficult situations,
we have the Word of God right in our hearts, ready to equip
us to make the right decisions and do the right things.

Do you feel equipped to fight the enemy?

Fearless

"Don't worry, because I am with you.
Don't be afraid, because I am your God.
I will make you strong and will help you.
I will support you with my right hand that saves you."

ISAIAH 41:10 ICB

Jocelyn lived in a house that had one bathroom all the way up on the third floor. Her room was in the basement, so whenever she needed to use the restroom in the middle of the night, she would have to go up all those stairs in the dark. Jocelyn was afraid of the dark but knew she had to make the trip. She remembered this verse that her dad had shared with her a few days ago during family Bible reading time. She didn't have to be afraid of the dark, or afraid of anything because the Holy Spirit was always with her.

What Jocelyn remembered is an important truth. If you believe in Jesus, he has given you the gift of the Holy Spirit, who is also fully God. He will comfort you and never leave you.

How can you be fearless?

Gift

It was only through this wonderful grace that we believed in him. Nothing we did could ever earn this salvation, for it was the gracious gift from God that brought us to Christ!

EPHESIANS 2:8 TPT

We mess up; it's part of life! As a human being, you have a sin nature. This means you will do things that break God's heart, the very things he asked you not to do. But God is so good. He has a big, huge gift waiting for you when you sin. It's called grace.

Grace is a gift we don't deserve because we are sinners. It's the good gift of us being forgiven. God gives us the good gift living with him forever simply because we believe in Jesus, and he is the King of our hearts. Grace is the wonderful way God shows us that he cares for us. And the best part is that it's a free gift. You can't earn it and you don't have to win it. Ask God today to show you his grace and take the good gift he has for you.

How do you feel about the gift of grace?

Hope

We are pressed on every side by troubles, but we are not
crushed. We are perplexed, but not driven to despair.
We are hunted down, but never abandoned by God.
We get knocked down, but we are not destroyed.

2 CORINTHIANS 4:8-9 NLT

The apostle Paul had a very hard life. He was shipwrecked,
beaten, and stoned. People hated him, and even his friends
sometimes left him all alone. He was often hungry, cold,
and tired. He spent time in prison and even years not being
allowed to leave his house. His friends had to bring him
food, or he couldn't eat!

Paul wrote in the Bible about having hope and joy. He
showed us that even when bad things happen, God still loves
us greatly, and we can always have hope in him. He cares
about what hurts you and is near when you cry. If you ever
feel like your life is too hard, cry out to God, and ask him to
help you. Tell him exactly how you are feeling. He wants to
know! He will never, ever leave you alone.

Where do you place your hope?

Identity

He saved us because of his mercy. It was not because of good
deeds we did to be right with him. He saved us through the
washing that made us new people through the Holy Spirit.

TITUS 3:5 NCV

Virginia always did the right thing. She turned in all her
homework on time; she was never late for class; she tried
not to hit her sister; and she never lied. She refused to cheat
on her math test even when Greg was going to give her the
answers, and she even helped a lost dog find his way home.
Shouldn't that be enough, she thought, to make God love me?

The truth is, Virginia didn't need to do any of those things
to make God love her because he already loved her more
than she could ever understand. He loved her even when she
didn't do any good things. Virginia's identity is tied to who
she is and not what she does. All she needs to do is believe in
Jesus and repent, and she is clean and new.

WhErE is youR identity?

Kindness

Be kind and affectionate toward one another. Has God graciously forgiven you? Then graciously forgive one another in the depths of Christ's love.

EPHESIANS 4:32 TPT

The words that her sister had said kept playing over and over again in her mind like a bad song on repeat. How could she be so mean? Zara rolled over on her bed and wiped her tears. She had just read in her Bible the night before about God's great forgiveness for her, but how could he expect her to forgive her sister for the mean things she said? It was so hard to forget! It was then that Zara realized forgetting may take time, but forgiveness can be now. Because God forgave her, he could also help her forgive her sister.

When someone hurts you, it's hard to forgive. Remember what God did for you in his kindness, and you can pass that same compassion along to others.

How can you show kindness to someone who has hurt you?

CReated

We are God's creation. He created us to belong to Christ
Jesus. Now we can do good works. Long ago God
prepared these works for us to do.

EPHESIANS 2:10 NIRV

Have you ever painted a picture that you were very proud
of? Maybe you are more into building, and you built the
most epic Lego tower. Or perhaps you crafted a friendship
bracelet from rubber bands that made you feel super proud.
Whatever you made, remember how proud you felt of your
creation?

Multiply that by infinity, and that's how much God loves you
and is proud of you—his very own creation. The Bible tells us
he knit each of us in our mother's womb. And he created all
of our parts, both the parts we like and the parts we don't like.
The next time you feel down about yourself, remember, you
are God's very good creation, and he loves every bit of you.

How does it feel to Know you weRe
specially cReated by God?

Life

"The thief's purpose is to steal and kill and destroy.
My purpose is to give them a rich and satisfying life."

JOHN 10:10 NLT

Sandra sighed loudly. The lock her dad had bought her for
her locker was gone. Someone had broken it and gotten into
her locker, then they had taken her brand-new jean jacket,
the one she had wanted so long with the smiley-face patch.
Being the victim of theft was a horrible feeling!

If you've ever had something stolen from you, you know
exactly how Sandra felt, and it's not good. Satan wants to
steal from us, but not just things like a jean jacket. He wants
to steal our love and peace and destroy our relationship with
God. We must live a life surrendered to Jesus, trusting in
him, and obeying his Word. That is how we let God protect
us from being a victim.

How can you keep your joy and peace?

Influence

Do not be fooled:
"Bad friends will ruin good habits."

1 CORINTHIANS 15:33 ICB

Tilly glanced longingly at the group of girls a few tables over. She wanted so badly to be their friend. They all seemed so, well, cool. They were popular, but Tilly knew what they did to become popular. They cheated on their schoolwork, they stole things from stores, and they said mean things about other people behind their backs. Even though all the kids seemed to like them, she knew that the teachers did not. Those girls were often rude and disrespectful to Ms. Smith, their homeroom teacher.

It was tempting to be popular, but Tilly knew the truth. If you hang out with people who have bad habits, you are far more likely to pick up those habits than change people. As a new follower of Jesus, she wanted to do what he said is right even if it meant not fitting in.

What good friends do you have?

Clean

All who make themselves clean from evil will be used for
special purposes. They will be made holy, useful to the
Master, ready to do any good work.

2 TIMOTHY 2:21 NCV

If you have to do chores at home, you've probably had to do
dishes. You could be lucky enough to have a dishwasher that
does some of the work for you. Have you ever loaded the
dishes, only to reach in the dishwasher the next day and still
find a dirty cup? Do you fill that cup with cool, clean water,
or do you wash it again?

Of course you don't use the dirty cup. That's gross! In the
same way, when we ask for forgiveness of our sins and we
believe in Jesus, God makes us clean. Now that we are clean,
our lives can be filled with his cool, refreshing presence so
that others may know him as well.

How clean is your cup?

Lovable

Since God loved us that much,
we surely ought to love each other.

1 JOHN 4:11 NLT

Do you have a special saying with your parents or grandparents regarding how much you love one another? Maybe you stretch your arms as wide as possible to show how much love you have. Maybe you have a special saying, like, " I love you to the moon and back!" You're trying to express with words how much love is between you.

How much does God love us? He loved us so much that he went to the greatest of lengths to make sure we could be with him forever. He sent his Son, Jesus, to sacrifice his life so we wouldn't have to die in our sins, and so we might be near God forever. Since he loves us that much, we can joyfully share that love with others.

How Lovable do you feel?

Growing

That will continue until we all become one in the faith.
We will also become one in the knowledge of God's Son.
Then we will be grown up in the faith.
We will receive everything that Christ has for us.

EPHESIANS 4:13 NIRV

"You are growing like a weed!" Charley's mom exclaimed.
Charley just grinned back at her mom. She was aware that
the shoes they bought a few months ago no longer fit, and
her ankles peaked out of the hem of her jeans. She knew her
mom didn't mind, and neither did she. Growing up meant
new privileges, new clothes, and mostly good things!

Did you know that just like our bodies grow, we are
supposed to grow in our faith too? Praying a prayer that you
believe in Jesus is not all there is to it. It also involves growth!
Reading your Bible, praying, and connecting with other
believers is how you grow as a Christian. When you grow,
Jesus has wonderful things promised for you. Growing up is
a great thing!

How are you growing in your faith?

ALERT

Pray in the Spirit at all times and on every occasion.
Stay alert and be persistent in your prayers
for all believers everywhere.

EPHESIANS 6:18 NLT

Have you ever tried to stay awake all night? It's not hard to stay up during normal hours, but once two or three in the morning comes, it can be pretty hard! Doing something at all times is impossible. How do we pray at all times and do other things like sleep? Is it even possible to stay awake to pray at all times?

The Bible isn't saying to pray and not do anything else. It's telling us to be aware of the presence of God at all times. We can be reassured that he is near when we need him, and when things overwhelm our minds, we can pray instead! We can welcome the presence of God at all times. We don't need to be in church to pray, and we don't need anyone else to lead us. Access to God is always available.

How can you be alert to what God is doing in and around you?

Peace

"I leave the gift of peace with you—my peace. Not the kind of fragile peace given by the world, but my perfect peace. Don't yield to fear or be troubled in your hearts— instead, be courageous!"

JOHN 14:27 TPT

Do you ever feel like everything is going wrong? Sometimes, things we cannot control make our hearts fill with anxiety and fear. Even your body can respond to fear, giving you butterflies in your stomach, tying it knots, or giving you headaches. It's important if you feel this way to tell someone about your fears, and who better to start with than God? He is the one in control, and he cares deeply for you.

When you feel anxious or afraid, pray to him and ask him to give you peace. Tell him what you're afraid of and ask him to help you trust him. It's also helpful if you tell someone you trust and let them pray for you as well! God has given you the gift of peace. Receive it today.

When do you feel the Most Peaceful?

Share

Don't forget to do good and to share with those in need.
These are the sacrifices that please God.

HEBREWS 13:16 NLT

Have you ever heard the phrase "Sharing is caring"? That is
a catchy rhyme to remind us of a truth from God's Word.
It can be easy to focus on only the things that you want,
like trying to earn enough money for a new bike or keeping
all your cool new toys safely put away where others can't
touch them.

The truth is, God has blessed you with many things. You
are not only blessed with physical things, but you are also
blessed with time, talent, wisdom, and so much more! Take
some time today to think about some of your blessings that
can be shared with others around you.

What can you share with someone this week?

Perfect

Christ suffered for our sins once for all time. He never sinned, but he died for sinners to bring you safely home to God. He suffered physical death, but he was raised to life in the Spirit.

1 PETER 3:18 NLT

No one likes to make mistakes, but everyone still does all the time. There is not one single person on this earth who is or has been perfect. You might look over at the girl in the desk next to you who has shiny hair and good grades and think she is perfect, but it's simply not true. We all mess up.

Even more than making mistakes, every single person on earth sins. To sin means that we do things that go against what God has said is right. The only person who has never sinned is Jesus. He is perfect. Because he is perfect, he is the only one who could create the bridge between us and God by sacrificing his life for us. Thank him for dying for your sins today.

What makes you perfect?

JUNE

"God is the one who saves me;
I will trust in him and not be afraid.
The LORD, the LORD gives me strength
and makes me sing.
He has saved me."

ISAIAH 12:2 NCV

Nourishing

"Anyone who eats my flesh and drinks my blood has eternal life, and I will raise that person on the last day."

JOHN 6:54 NLT

Is this really in the Bible? What can they possibly be talking about: eating flesh and drinking blood? This sounds more like a vampire story than something coming out of the mouth of Jesus, doesn't it? It's not a weird story; this is actually good news for you.

Jesus bled on the cross for our sins. We remember this act by taking what is called communion, (the small crackers or bread and juice or wine) that you see at church sometimes. When people take communion, they are remembering that Jesus gave his life so we could be free from sin and live forever with him. This is true nourishment for your soul.

How do you REMEMBER what Jesus did foR you oN the cRoss?

Eternity

"Martha," Jesus said, "You don't have to wait until then.
I am the Resurrection, and I am Life Eternal. Anyone who
clings to me in faith, even though he dies, will live forever.
And the one who lives by believing in me will never die.
Do you believe this?"

JOHN 11:25-26 TPT

Andrea's mom had made a colorful paper chain to help her
count down the days to her birthday. It felt like an eternity
until her birthday would arrive. She knew it was only one
month away, yet it was impossible to be patient. She whined
to her mom that it was taking forever though she knew it
actually wasn't. Forever was not a concept she could really
wrap her mind around.

Did you know that having faith in Jesus means you will live
forever? Our faith gives us many good things, and one of
those is the guarantee that we will be with God for eternity.
It's hard for our minds to understand this, but that should
just make us worship God more. He is wiser and stronger
than we know.

How do you feel about eternity?

Qualified

It is not that we think we are qualified to do anything on our own. Our qualification comes from God.

2 CORINTHIANS 3:5 NLT

Sometimes when Jennifer read the Bible, she felt like she wasn't good enough to be a Christian. She didn't have much to offer God, and she wasn't good at remembering the rules. One Wednesday night, she told her youth pastor these things. The pastor reminded her that she was valuable and important to God. He said it is not because of anything we do that makes us special; God loves us no matter what.

Every talent, skill, or resource you have is a gift from God. Salvation also is a gift that you can't earn on your own. You are qualified to be a believer because of what Jesus did on the cross, so stop worrying. Stop trying so hard to make God like you and remember that he already does.

How do you qualify to be a believer?

Ready

"You also must be ready.
The Son of Man will come at an hour
when you don't expect him."

MATTHEW 24:44 NIRV

Everything Connie was attempting to do was taking twice as long because she kept stopping to look out the window. She was trying to clean her room and couldn't help but sneak another peak. Her grandpa and grandma were coming for a visit. They lived in another country, so their visits were extra special. Each time they came, they packed one special suitcase full of exotic candy and gifts. She was full of anticipation for their arrival.

The Bible tells us that no one knows the day or the hour when Jesus will return. All believers are waiting and hoping for him to return soon. Everyone is very excited that he will make things right. We can get ready for his return by learning more about God's character, telling others about him, and spending time reading his Word.

How ready are you for Jesus to return?

Example

"I did this as an example
so that you should do as I have done for you."

JOHN 13:15 NCV

Sheri loved to play *Simon Says*. Every time Mr. Smith suggested they play at recess, Sheri was the first to volunteer. She loved trying to trick people into getting out. She watched carefully to make sure everyone followed her example and did the exact motions that she did. If anyone messed up, she quickly pointed it out. Her best friend, Jane, was usually the last one to be out. She knew Sheri so well that she could guess exactly what she was going to do.

Because Jane was such good friends with Sheri, she could anticipate her motions. When you spend time with someone, you grow in your relationship with them. You get to know them well. The more we get to know Jesus, the more like him we become. We follow his example and lead others to life in him.

How do you follow Jesus' example?

Constant

Jesus Christ is the same
yesterday and today and forever.

HEBREWS 13:8 NIRV

Aubrey just learned that she would be switching schools
in the fall. She sat down on her front stoop and sighed.
Everything felt like it was changing so fast! Her aunt and
uncle moved away, and now this. Although she felt sad, she
remembered what her aunt told her before she left. Aunt
Rachel loved Jesus a lot and reminded Aubrey that she could
always rely on him. She reminded her of a verse in Hebrews
that tells us how Jesus stays the same. That means his
character never changes. He was good before, and he will be
good tomorrow and forever. He was full of grace yesterday,
and he will be tomorrow and forever.

All the wonderful things that Jesus is, he will always be. You
can always rely on him because he is constant.

How does it make you feel knowing that Jesus is constant?

Treasures

"Don't store up treasures here on earth, where moths eat them and rust destroys them, and where thieves break in and steal. Store your treasures in heaven, where moths and rust cannot destroy, and thieves do not break in and steal."

MATTHEW 6:19-20 NLT

Evelyn couldn't wait to grow up. She loved to think about how she would have her very own house and paint all the walls pink. She would fill it with funky furniture and put chocolate milk in the fridge. She would have a whole wall just for rollerblades, and buckets of candy on her counters. Being a grownup was going to be great!

What does the Bible mean by storing up all your treasures on earth? It means you are focused on all the things you can get while you live here. But if you focus on just yourself and the things of this earth, you will miss out on all God has to offer. Material things won't last forever. God has things to offer that will.

What are your very best treasures?

ONLY

Serve only the LORD your God and fear him alone.
Obey his commands, listen to his voice, and cling to him.

DEUTERONOMY 13:4 NLT

On the third day of summer camp was the obstacle course
challenge. Each cabin selected one camper to run through
the whole course—blindfolded. Becky was selected to
compete for Cabin 3. When the director shouted, "Go!" she
took a few hesitant steps forward. It was harder with the
blindfold! All the cabins shouted at their campers, trying
to help them, but the directions became a jumbled mess
of voices. If she really focused in, Becky could hear her
counselor's voice above the others. She knew if she listened
to her, she would make it through the obstacles.

When you follow Jesus, it can feel like going through an
obstacle course blindfolded. There will be many voices
shouting directions. Some might seem good, but they
aren't meant for you. Some will lead you way off track. It's
important to focus on God's voice and follow him only. He
will get you safely where you need to go.

How can you hear only God's voice above the others?

Give

Tell them to use their money to do good. They should be rich in good works and generous to those in need, always being ready to share with others.

1 TIMOTHY 6:18 NLT

Miya was brand new to gymnastics. At her weekly practice, there were gymnasts of all skill levels. She watched in awe as the older girls flipped their bodies around the slim bar. One time, she tried to lift herself up on the bar, but she couldn't even get her head above it. An older girl saw her and said gently, "It takes practice; start with the lower bar. You're not quite strong enough to lift your whole body yet."

When you exercise, your muscles become stronger. You don't start out with the heaviest weight or the hardest activity. You start small and work your way up. Giving to others is the same. The more you practice, the better you will become at it. No matter how small an amount you have, practice being generous and ask God to guide you on how much to give.

What can you give someone today?

Changed

Bodies made of flesh and blood can't share in the kingdom of God. And what dies can't share in what never dies. Listen! I am telling you a mystery. We will not all die. But we will all be changed. That will happen in a flash, as quickly as you can wink an eye. It will happen at the blast of the last trumpet.

1 CORINTHIANS 15:50-52 NIRV

Jada had just purchased a new notebook. The cover of the notebook was special. If you turned it slightly one direction, the image changed. She moved her notebook back and forth, watching the image of space change to a spaceship and astronauts. Jada was enthralled by the changing image and the shiny surface of the notebook. It was almost too cool to even write in!

The Bible tells us that Jesus is going to make everything new. When he comes back, he will make everything perfect again. God meant for our world to be perfect, but sin changed everything. When Jesus comes back, there will be no more tears, no sickness, and no pain. Even your body will be made new. What a wonderful promise!

What changes are you excited for?

Sympathy

All of you should be in agreement,
understanding each other, loving each other as family,
being kind and humble.

1 PETER 3:8 NCV

Melody walked into the kitchen, and immediately she could tell something was wrong. She automatically assumed that her mom was upset with her for leaving the milk out. "Sorry, Mom!" she said, and grabbed the milk to put it away. Her mom looked up, distracted. "Why are you sorry?" she asked Melody. Melody held up the milk, but her mom said, "Oh no, honey! This had nothing to do with you. I'm upset because I didn't get the job." Melody realized she had assumed the wrong thing. She gave her mom a hug.

We often assume everything is about us. To show sympathy means thinking about others first and not assuming that we know how they feel or why. It is important to listen before we speak, and to humbly remember that we need be aware of others.

How can you show sympathy today?

Suffer

In his kindness God called you to share in his eternal glory by means of Christ Jesus. So after you have suffered a little while, he will restore, support, and strengthen you, and he will place you on a firm foundation.

1 PETER 5:10 NLT

Olivia knew her parents were having a hard time. They often seemed sad, frustrated, and stressed. They talked in hushed whispers, and she saw them crying occasionally. One day, she asked her dad about it. Her dad gave her a hug and thanked her for asking. He then said that even though things were very tough this year, he knew that they would be okay because of their faith in Jesus.

Everyone will experience suffering. It can be painful, and we often have no control over it. Thankfully, those who follow Jesus know that suffering will not last forever. Jesus is going to make all things new. He always keeps his promises, and this hope helps us endure. Instead of setting your sights on what is hard, set your focus on the hope that is to come.

What things are you suffering through right now?

Power

We now have this light shining in our hearts, but we ourselves are like fragile clay jars containing this great treasure. This makes it clear that our great power is from God, not from ourselves.

2 CORINTHIANS 4:7 NLT

Claire tried to be perfect at everything she did. She didn't know why, but it felt very satisfying to get things just right. In her schoolwork, artwork, and daily habits, she needed everything to be just so. Achieving this made her feel in control. Her parents noticed this about her and sat her down to talk. They reminded her that only God is perfect, and that it takes trust to let go and allow God to be in control. Claire knew they were right and prayed for help.

Being a believer in Jesus is not about being perfect. Every single person makes mistakes and has flaws, yet God has none. We shouldn't focus on our own flaws or the flaws of others, but instead remember how great it is that we serve a perfect God. His power is shown when he is strong in our weakness.

How is God's power shown in you?

Sacrifice

We see Jesus, who as a man, lived for a short time lower
than the angels and has now been crowned with
glorious honor because of what he suffered in his death.
For it was by God's grace that he experienced death's
bitterness on behalf of everyone! For now he towers above all
creation, for all things exist through him and for him.

HEBREWS 2:9-10 TPT

Liza sat quietly in the back of the sanctuary as the worship
band continued to play. They had a special night of prayer
and worship, and for the first time she felt like she really
understood what Jesus had done for her. She saw the
sacrifice Jesus made for her. She felt loved by him and in awe
of how he pursued her. She knew she wanted to follow Jesus
forever. She sat for a while more, journaling and thanking
God for opening her eyes.

A sacrifice is when you give something up. Jesus sacrificed
everything so that we could be with God. He is the reason
we are saved. Our sins are completely wiped clean because of
his sacrifice.

How can you thank Jesus for his sacrifice today?

Listen

My dear brothers, always be willing to listen
and slow to speak. Do not become angry easily.

JAMES 1:19 ICB

Whenever Violet and Laurel fought, things became very
loud. Violet felt out of control as she continued to raise her
voice. Laurel did not want to hear what her sister had to say;
she only wanted her sister to know how right she was. Her
mom sat both of them down during their latest argument.
After both girls had calmed down, her mom read James 1:19
from the Bible. She explained to them how God wants us to
love others and one way of doing that is to truly listen.

Being slow to speak means you have ears that are open as
you try to understand the other person. If you have a hard
time listening to others, pray to God for help in controlling
your tongue. When you find yourself getting upset, take time
to become calm and try to hear the other person's side.

Who could you try to listen to better?

Dance

Break forth with dancing!
Make music and sing God's praises
with the rhythm of the drums!

PSALM 149:3 TPT

Ivy followed all the rules. She spent a lot of time worrying about whether or not she had forgotten anything. Even though she kept a good handle on things, she realized one day that she did not enjoy it. She was uptight and stressed most days. There really wasn't a lot of fun in her life. When Ms. Frank read today's verse in her Sunday school class, she realized what had been missing. It never occurred to her that God could dance and be happy.

Sometimes it feels like Christianity is just a long list of rules. Maybe you've understood it as something you suffer through or a place you have to be serious. Christianity is supposed to be full of joy. God wants us to celebrate the new life we have been given and live in freedom from sin. This should make us want to dance.

What can you dance about today?

Amazing

In the middle of them was someone who looked like a son of man. He was dressed in a long robe with gold strip of cloth around his chest. The hair on his head was white like wool, as white as snow. His eyes were like a blazing fire. His feet were like bronze metal glowing in a furnace. His voice sounded like rushing waters. He held seven stars in his right hand.

REVELATION 1:13-15 NIRV

Sondra flipped through the pages of the photo album one more time. She loved looking through the pictures of her mom and her mom's brother. Uncle Neal lived in a different country, so she had never met him. For the very first time, they were taking a trip to see him. She had heard so much about him that she felt like they had met, but she was excited to see him for real.

It can be hard to know someone if you have never met them in person. We have never seen Jesus, but one day we will see him face-to-face. We will no longer have to imagine what he looks like. What an amazing day that will be!

How amazed do you think you will be when you see Jesus?

Watchful

Be alert. Continue strong in the faith.
Have courage, and be strong.
Do everything in love.

1 CORINTHIANS 16:13-14 NCV

Johanna was going camping with her whole family. All
the parents were busy setting up the tents, so they asked
Johanna and her older cousins if they could keep an eye on
the younger ones. She and her cousin needed to stay alert,
counting the younger kids and watching them carefully to
make sure they were all there. She knew it was important to
stay focused, so no one got lost.

Just like Johanna needed to be alert so others were safe, it is
important as a Christian to pay attention to what is going on
around you. Your life will be full of choices to serve God or
serve the world. You must remain watchful of what is going
on, so you continue to make good choices.

What are you watchful of in your life?

Known

"I knew you before I formed you in your mother's womb.
Before you were born I set you apart
and appointed you as my prophet to the nations."

JEREMIAH 1:5 NLT

Every year at the beginning of the school year, Caroline enjoyed filling out a special booklet. In the booklet there were many questions about who she was and the things she liked. It made her feel important to write down all the things, and she felt proud to show it to her parents. She loved the feeling of being known and understood by others.

Do you know who knows you perfectly? God does. There is no part of you that is a mystery to him. He created all of you and knows the deepest parts of you. Whenever you feel misunderstood, remember that God always understands. He is your closest friend, and you can share anything with him. He knows you better than you know yourself!

How does it feel to know you are truly known by God?

Persistent

Rejoice in our confident hope.
Be patient in trouble,
and keep on praying.

ROMANS 12:12 NLT

Bethany loved to run, so her mom suggested she join the track team at school. At her first practice, she decided to sign up to run the long-distance marathon. She trained every day and worked very hard. At practice, her coach liked to tell the students that all they had to do was take one more step than the day before. Each small step would add up to finishing the long race. Her coach encouraged them that they could do far more than they thought they could if they didn't give up.

The advice that Bethany's coach gave was good advice for our Christian walk as well. The goal is to follow after Jesus for our whole lives. It is important to develop persistence, so we never give up. Every small action, each prayer, whenever we read the Bible or choose to do things God's way is another step in our journey of following him.

How persistent are you?

Prize

I do not mean that I am already as God wants me to be. I have not yet reached that goal. But I continue trying to reach it and to make it mine. Christ wants me to do that. That is the reason Christ made me his. Brothers, I know that I have not yet reached that goal. But there is one thing I always do: I forget the things that are past. I try as hard as I can to reach the goal that is before me.

PHILIPPIANS 3:12-13 ICB

Every year Lorelei's church held a carnival. The best part was that everything was free! You could play all the games, eat cotton candy, and climb the rock wall! At each place, you earned tickets that you could redeem at the prize booth. There were many cool toys and candy in that booth. Lorelei had her eyes set on a scooter that was worth fifty tickets. She was motivated to complete all the games so she could get that prize.

When we follow Jesus, the prize that motivates us to keep going is that we will spend eternity with God. What we do now on earth will affect how we live in eternity. Though we might face troubles now, continuing to follow Jesus through those hard times is worth it.

Do you have your eyes set on the final prize?

Offering

Since God has shown us great mercy, I beg you to offer your lives as a living sacrifice to him. Your offering must be only for God and pleasing to him.

ROMANS 12:1 NCV

Jillian's knew her friends always had her back. Her best friend, Sam, had proven this from the very beginning. It was a small thing, but one that made a big impact. On their first day of school in second grade she couldn't get her milk carton open. She was sitting two seats down from Sam who kindly took her milk carton and opened it for her. From that day on, Sam opened Jillian's milk cartons. She was so grateful for the kindness he showed her that she wanted to show him kindness in return.

Opening someone else's milk might seem like a small thing, but it is a kindness that can mean a lot. When someone does something kind, it is nice to return the favor. God has been so kind to us. He sent Jesus to die on the cross so our sin would be wiped clean. He gives us mercy, grace, and so much more.

What can you offer God to return his kindness?

Wise

Listen to me and you will be prudent and wise.
For even the foolish and feeble can receive an understanding
heart that will change their inner being.

PROVERBS 8:5 TPT

Lucy had an early morning bus to catch which would be
taking her to the statewide track meet. The night before, she
had been invited to Nichole's sleepover birthday party. Lucy
wanted to go so badly. She talked it over with her mom,
knowing that she wouldn't get any sleep if she went to the
sleepover. Her mom left the decision up to her, telling her
to use wisdom. She knew that it would be wiser to get good
sleep for her meet, so she chose to go to the party but to also
leave at a reasonable time.

To have wisdom means that you know how to apply truth
to your life and use good judgment. The Bible speaks about
wisdom often, comparing it to a treasure we should eagerly
seek. Wisdom has nothing to do with talent, skill, or being
born into the right family. This is a treasure that all can have.
We just have to ask God for it.

What do you need wisdom for today?

Repent

Repent of your sins and turn to God, so that your sins may
be wiped away. Then times of refreshment will come from
the presence of the Lord, and he will again send you Jesus,
your appointed Messiah.

ACTS 3:19-20 NLT

Imagine getting into a big fight with a friend. You call your
friend mean names and things don't go well. After you cool
off and recognize what you did wrong, you go apologize.
Instead of apologizing to your friend, you apologize to
your mom. Wait, that doesn't make sense! Why would you
apologize to your mom when it was your friend you hurt?
It only works to apologize if you're speaking to the right
person.

To repent means to turn from our sins. God is the only one
who can forgive all of our sins. Though we should apologize
to the person who was hurt, when we do something wrong,
we should also repent to God. None of our mistakes can
keep us from him. He is always waiting and willing to forgive
us. Asking for forgiveness from him is the only way to
experience true freedom.

Is there something you need to repent of today?

ReLevant

All Scripture is inspired by God and is useful for teaching,
for showing people what is wrong in their lives, for
correcting faults, and for teaching how to live right.

2 TIMOTHY 3:16 NCV

Genevieve reached for her Bible. She had been taught
about the benefits of reading God's Word. She knew how
encouraging it could be. Sometimes she found it boring, and
she felt guilty about that. She didn't understand parts that
were confusing, and she didn't know what they had to do
with her. She felt conflicted.

You may have been raised learning all about the Bible, or
maybe you've recently picked it up. No matter how much
knowledge you have, there is always something more to
learn in the Bible. It will always be relevant. God's Word is a
wonderful gift to help us live a life that pleases him. If you're
having a hard time with your Bible reading, ask God to make
it come alive to you.

What ScRiptuRes have you Read RecentLy that seem ReLevant?

FRiendship

"I don't call you servants now. A servant does not know what his master is doing. But now I call you friends because I have made known to you everything I heard from my Father."

JOHN 15:15 ICB

Isabella and her sister were watching her favorite show on TV. It was a singing competition with her favorite musical artist as a judge. When the show was over, they talked about how fashionable and cool the artist was. They daydreamed about being friends with her, wondering what it would be like to hangout and sing together.

Have you ever daydreamed about being friends with a famous actor, musician, or athlete? Does it seem a little farfetched? Did you know that the Creator of the entire world is your friend? God is stronger, wiser, more talented, and richer than you can ever imagine, and he wants to be with you. He calls you his friend.

Do you know that God is your friend?

Glorious

On the glorious splendor of your majesty,
and on your wondrous works, I will meditate.

PSALM 145:5 NLT

Macy took a break from homework to go for a walk. Earlier that week, her Bible study teacher had challenged them to go on a prayer walk to appreciate the glory of God. A prayer walk is when you walk somewhere while praying. Macy's prayer walk was to specifically focus on God's greatness through nature. She marveled at the details of the smallest flowers and felt the breeze through the trees. This led to her thinking about the one who had created them all.

God is striking in beauty and splendor. He is worthy of being admired and praised. We live in a very distracted and busy world in which people rarely take the time to seek God. Slowing down and taking a walk or being in nature can help us remember how glorious God is.

What things remind you of God's glory?

Obedient

As you deal with one another, you should think and act as Jesus did. In his very nature he was God. Jesus was equal with God. But Jesus didn't take advantage of that fact. Instead, he made himself nothing. He did this by taking on the nature of a servant. He was made just like human beings. He appeared as a man. He was humble and obeyed God completely. He did this even though it led to his death.

PHILIPPIANS 2:5-8 NIRV

Chloe had just read through the Ten Commandments. Some of them seemed easy to obey, like not murdering. But others, like not lying and honoring her parents, seemed a little overwhelming. There was a lot to keep track of, and she was unsure if she could make the right choices. When she told her father, he told her not to become overwhelmed, but to follow the example of Jesus.

Sometimes the Bible seems like a ton of rules. You may worry about keeping them all straight. If you worry about being obedient to God, let him calm your heart. Focus on following the example of Jesus. Ask the Holy Spirit to help you and guide you into obedience.

How can you be obedient to God?

Dependent

The LORD is good to those who depend on him,
to those who search for him.
So it is good to wait quietly
for salvation from the LORD.

LAMENTATIONS 3:25-26 NLT

Nala's dad was in the military, which meant they moved every two years. By now, she was a pro at packing up her boxes and getting everything ready. This was the first move her little sister would remember though. She was worried that all her dolls would not make it to the new house. Nala reminded her that they had done this before, and the moving company had always gotten their things there. She didn't need to worry because they were dependable movers.

When you depend on someone, it means you trust or rely on them. Nala's family relied on the moving company to get their things safely from one house to another. When we depend on God, we trust that he will do what he says he will do. We know that we can count on him to keep his promises. Our hearts are free of anxiety and worry because we know that he will always come through for us.

How are you depending on God right now?

Judge

Whenever the LORD raised up a judge over Israel, he was with that judge and rescued the people from their enemies throughout the judge's lifetime. For the LORD took pity on his people, who were burdened by oppression and suffering.

JUDGES 2:18 NLT

Zuri listened to the adults talk in her family's sunroom. Many of them seemed to be speaking about the government. Most seemed frustrated, some were happy, but more were annoyed. She didn't understand the exact things they talked about, but she asked her parents if she should be worried. Her parents told her that no matter who is in control of the government, God is still King of everything. No one can take the throne from him, and he will never lose his authority.

No matter what country you live in or how great or evil your leader is, God is always greater. God is for his people, and he is in control of all. The only one who judges everyone is God. We can trust that he is powerful enough to accomplish his will. He is faithful to those who serve and love him.

How grateful are you that God is the judge?

Inheritance

It is by his great mercy that we have been born again. Now we live with great expectation, and we have a priceless inheritance—an inheritance that is kept in heaven for you, pure and undefiled, beyond the reach of change and decay.

1 PETER 1:4 NLT

Jana's grandpa owned a thirty-acre farm that she had grown up on. It had rolling hills and tall trees, a small pond, and a barn to play in. As she, her dad, and her grandpa sat at the back of the property, her grandpa took her hand. He told her how one day all this land would be hers. First it would become her dad's, and then it would be hers. It was important to grandpa that the land stay in the family.

An inheritance is something that is given from one person to the next. Usually when someone dies, their land, their belongings, or their money is passed on to their spouse or children. It's a gift from someone who loves you and wants to take care of you. Just like Jana will inherit land from her family, those in God's family inherit all that he has.

What part of your Godly inheritance are you excited about?

JULY

He gives strength
to those who are tired
and more power
to those who are weak.

Isaiah 40:29 NCV

Justified

Since we have been made right with God by our faith,
we have peace with God. This happened through
our Lord Jesus Christ.

ROMANS 5:1 NCV

Cynthia had been invited to church by her neighbor Janice.
She was the only one in her family to attend every Sunday.
It had been about two years now that Janice and her family
would swing by and pick Cynthia up. Sometimes the teacher
used big words she had never heard before, words like
justification. Janice's mom took extra time on the way home
to answer Cynthia's questions.

The words you hear or read in the Bible can seem
complicated. To be justified is a legal term meaning someone
is right. When we stand before God, as his believers, we are
declared good. God is perfect and cannot have sin in his
presence, but we are justified because of what Jesus did on
the cross.

What does justification mean to you?

Faithful

All the LORD's ways are loving and faithful
toward those who obey what his covenant commands.

PSALM 25:10 NIRV

Camila sprinted towards the ball. She successfully kicked it away from the oncoming player, passing it to one of her forwards. As she jogged back to her position, she could hear her family cheering for her. She blushed a bit but smiled. Her family was so encouraging and supportive, and they made sure to be at every one of her games. She knew they were her biggest fans. Their excitement for her made her want to do her very best, but she also knew if she messed up, they would encourage her to try again.

God is a faithful fan of yours. He is on your side, wanting to help you and guide through everything you face. He encourages and comforts you through the Holy Spirit. He is so proud that you are his daughter. He is cheering for you no matter what happens.

How has God been faithful to you?

Result

You have been set free from sin. God has made you
his slaves. The benefit you gain leads to holy living.
And the end result is eternal life.

ROMANS 6:22 NIRV

Gabriella picked up the last piece of trash from her sister's
car. She had washed the outside and wiped down the inside
too. Her sister had promised to take her to a movie if she
cleaned her car. She looked all through her house, but she
could not find her sister. She glanced at her watch, knowing
the movie started soon. There was still no sign of her sister. It
seems she had tricked her. Gabriella felt frustrated. She had
done the work, and now she wanted the reward.

If you choose to spend your life following Jesus, your reward
is a sure thing! God doesn't ask us to do what is right and
follow his Word, and then not reward us. He is not trying
to trick us, use us, or hide from us. The result of our trust in
him is getting to spend eternity with him.

What Result are you Looking Forward to?

FREEDOM

Let me be clear, the Anointed One has set us free—
not partially, but completely and wonderfully free!
We must always cherish this truth and stubbornly refuse
to go back into the bondage of our past.

GALATIANS 5:1 TPT

Maria and her older brother loved watching funny videos on the computer. They watched a clip about a group of people trying to help a sheep. The poor farm animal had walked into a ditch and had gotten stuck. The people freed him, but then the sheep ran a few feet and jumped right back into the ditch! It was hilarious to Maria. The sheep did this three times until it finally ran in another direction. Maria and her brother hit play again, laughing.

The Bible tells us we have been set free from sin! If we have been set free, why would we jump back into our old sins? Just like the sheep that kept jumping back into its self-inflicted trap, we can sometimes forget our freedom and keep returning to our old patterns of behavior. We need to remember that Christ died so we could be free.

How can you show your thankfulness for your freedom?

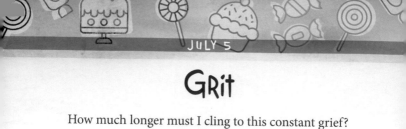

Grit

How much longer must I cling to this constant grief?
I've endured this shaking of my soul.
So how much longer will my enemy have the upper hand?
It's been long enough!

PSALM 13:2 TPT

Josefina was supposed to practice her violin for twenty minutes every day. Some days she enjoyed it; others she really didn't want to spend the time. On those days, she would set her timer, but then she would fiddle around or take a long time picking out the sheet music. She would move slowly enough to make it seem like she had practiced, but she really wasn't. She didn't know that this made other practice days harder.

When you choose to follow Jesus, there will be days when you are tempted to give up. You will need grit. This means that you continue even when it gets hard. You are the only one who can choose to persevere or give up. It's not always comfortable or easy to do what Jesus asks. Ask Jesus to help you have grit today.

What does gRit Look Like to you?

Happy

I realize that the best thing for them is to be happy and enjoy themselves as long as they live. God wants all people to eat and drink and be happy in their work, which are gifts from God.

ECCLESIASTES 3:12-13 NCV

Teresa loved cheerleading. She and her friends had been on the school team since second grade. No one had to try out. As they went into junior high school, they would have to try out for the team. Suddenly, things began to change in her group of friends. Everyone was stressed out about cheerleading. There were fights and bickering about who would make the team. No one enjoyed themselves since they were all competing for a spot. Teresa felt sad. They had forgotten how happy they felt when they cheered together.

God wants us to enjoy our lives. He is full of joy, and he wants to share that with us. This isn't a guarantee that we will have an easy life, but God wants us to have the joy that only he can give. When you find your happiness in God, everything else fades in importance.

How can you have a happy day?

Sing

Sing to him. Sing praise to him.
Tell about all the wonderful things he has done.

1 CHRONICLES 16:9 NIRV

It was the last night of summer camp for Veronica. Every morning and evening that week, all the campers had gathered for prayer and worship. Veronica loved singing the songs. Tonight however, the worship leader asked everyone to sing their own song to the Lord. As others around her lifted their voices with their own words, Veronica thought it sounded beautiful. But she didn't know what to sing. What if she said the wrong thing?

You don't have to be a performing artist to sing praise to God. You don't have to know the right words or sing in tune. Just sing whatever is on your mind and in your heart. Your worship is important to him. He isn't worried about you singing the right thing. He just loves your praise.

Can you sing your own song to God today?

DEVELOP

We can rejoice, too, when we run into problems and trials,
for we know that they help us develop endurance. And
endurance develops strength of character, and character
strengthens our confident hope of salvation.

ROMANS 5:3-4 NLT

Amelia was listening to her cousin tell all about his
competition. A radio station was giving away a car. Everyone
who wanted to win the car had to come to the radio station
and put a hand on the car. They had to keep one hand on
the car at all times, day and night, until there was a winner.
Amelia's cousin made it forty-eight hours before he let go,
yet there were still people there with their hands on the car!
Amelia marveled at their endurance.

When things don't go as we plan, it's easy to be frustrated.
Things don't go as we want them to, so we want to give up.
The Bible tells us that we will have trials. That makes them
a normal part of life. Trials help us develop endurance,
meaning we will keep going even when things are hard. You
can't always control situations, but you can control your
attitude and your decisions.

What character would you like God to develop in you?

WORK

Lazy people want much but get little,
but those who work hard will prosper.

PROVERBS 13:4 NLT

Every Saturday morning, Harper and her family did their chores. Mom set out a list and appointed tasks. Then they blasted some fun music and got to work. Harper marveled at how much faster the work went when the whole family did it together. She was tired, but she felt accomplished when the house smelled good, and everything was in its place. Her dad always rewarded them with a heaping Saturday brunch of waffles and bacon.

When God made the whole world, he rested on the seventh day. He created us to need rest as well. Rest is a wonderful gift from God. We are not made to keep going 24-7 like a toy that never turns off. Rest helps us to recharge and remember that God is in control. When you work hard, rest can be so sweet, and that is how God intended it to be.

What hard work have you done lately?

Teach

My brothers, I am sure that you are full of goodness.
I know that you have all the knowledge you need
and that you are able to teach each other.

ROMANS 15:14 ICB

Luna loved youth group. Every Wednesday night they gathered in the church basement. Some of her closest friends were there, and they would play games and learn about Jesus. She had two youth leaders, and she really liked them both. Mr. James was funny and told the best stories, and Ms. Karen always had a listening ear. They both made everyone who came to youth group feel loved and valued. They showed through their actions what a Christian really is.

We teach people about Jesus by the way we live. Others can see Jesus through us when we follow his example. It is a bit like the moon. The moon reflects the sun to give light to the earth at night. We are to reflect Christ so we can teach the world about him. We can use our attitudes and our actions to show people what God is like.

Who can you teach about Jesus?

PONDER

Continue to think about the things that are good and worthy of praise. Think about the things that are true and honorable and right and pure and beautiful and respected.

PHILIPPIANS 4:8 ICB

Avery had been staring at her phone for a long time. She started out watching one short video, then another, then another. Soon it was two hours later. Avery felt kind of gross. She hadn't eaten anything bad, but staring at that screen for so long made her feel icky. Some videos were funny, some were informative, and some she knew she probably shouldn't have watched. She decided to delete the app and take a break. She put down her phone, picked up her basketball, and wandered outside.

The things you ponder can have power over you. What you put into your mind is important. Other people may not know what you watch, listen to, read, or think about, but these things have the power to impact your life. You are responsible for being the gatekeeper of what you let in and controlling what you think about.

What good things will you ponder today?

True

Love must be honest and true.
Hate what is evil.
Hold on to what is good.

ROMANS 12:9 NIV

Eleanor noticed that her cat was not his usual spunky self. He was lying listlessly in a corner. She continued to watch him and noticed he didn't eat or drink anything all day. Eleanor was worried about him, so she told her mom what she had observed. Her mom called the vet. The vet told them to bring the cat in, so Eleanor gently placed him in his carrier and drove with her mom to the clinic. She really hoped the vet could tell them what was wrong.

When your pet is sick, you call the vet. If you want to understand math, you ask a math teacher. When your parent's car breaks down, they call a mechanic. When you need help with something, it makes sense to find an expert. The Bible tells us that God is love. He is the expert. If you want to understand love, you need to get to know God. He cannot do anything unloving. He can teach you what true love looks like.

What kind of Love is true Love?

LeaRN

Do what you learned and received from me,
what I told you, and what you saw me do.
And the God who gives peace will be with you.

PHILIPPIANS 4:9 NCV

Scarlett had been a part of the Big Brothers Big Sisters of America program for three years. When she first started, they had paired her up with an older girl named Aria. Scarlett loved to hang out with her. Aria played soccer for her college, so she taught Scarlett how to become a better goalie. She taught her how to paint her nails, and they learned about camping. Aria had many skills she passed onto Scarlett, but she also gave her advice and guidance on how to be kind and generous. These were qualities that Scarlett saw Aria display in her own life.

There will be many people in your life from whom you can learn. God knows what you need and will use other people as teachers. When these good examples come into your life, pay attention. Listen to what they have to say and humbly learn as much as you can.

What caN you LeaRN today?

SUPPORT

Insult your Creator, will you?
That's exactly what you do every time
that you oppress the powerless!
Showing kindness to the poor is equal
to honoring your maker.

PROVERBS 14:31 TPT

Layla turned the corner at school. She noticed a girl who had dropped all her books. The bell rang, and all the other students rushed past her, scattering her papers and pencils even more. No one stopped to try to help. Layla made her way through the crowd and began to pick up the papers. The girl looked up in awe. It was like no one had ever helped her before. For the rest of the day, Layla thought about that small action, and how much it had seemed to mean to the girl.

When you treat other people the way you want to be treated, you bring honor to God. Being a Christian is not about trying to gain knowledge of God or understanding of the Bible. Those are good things, but we have to let those good things impact our actions. God wants us to show his love. He wants you to befriend the lonely, and support those who are down.

Who can you support today?

Royalty

"You have made them members of a royal family.
You have made them priests to serve our God.
They will rule on the earth."

REVELATION 5:10 NIRV

Penelope loved going to her extended family's annual picnic.
She knew how blessed she was to be in this family. When
they arrived at the picnic, there were always big hugs and
laughter. Everyone caught up with what was going on in
while they ate delicious hamburgers and big salads. She
always felt loved. Her favorite part of the day was when her
great-grandparents prayed over each child. That was a huge
blessing.

You may come from a family that makes you feel loved,
or you may not. If you ever feel like you don't belong,
remember that God the Father calls you his child. You
belong to his family forever, and that makes you royalty. You
are the daughter of the King! If you feel lonely, ask God to
help you know how loved and cherished you are by him.

How does it feel to be Royalty?

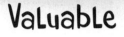

Valuable

Who can find an excellent woman?
She is worth far more than rubies.

PROVERBS 31:10 NIRV

Zoe listened carefully to the instructor at the museum. He was a geologist, and he was explaining to the group what made a rock valuable. He explained how you could find many different rocks on the coast, but only certain ones with certain qualities were valuable to sell. He held up many examples and Zoe found his talk fascinating. She was ready to hit the shore and try to find valuable rocks.

What makes a woman excellent? The most important quality is her love for Jesus. It's honoring to God when she has dedicated her life to serving him. She loves others with her actions in order to bring God glory. This is the type of woman we should hope to become.

In what areas do you feel most valuable?

WELCOME

Remember to welcome strangers, because some who have
done this have welcomed angels without knowing it.

HEBREWS 13:2 NCV

Amber sat in her usual spot on the school bus. Glancing up,
she noticed an unfamiliar face walking down the aisle. As the
girl passed open seat after open seat, no one made room for
her. The girl looked unsure and nervous. As she approached
Amber, Amber offered her the seat next to her. They talked
the entire bus ride. The girl explained how her dad had lost
his job, so they had to move in with her grandparents for a
while. She was new in town and sad about the move. Amber
was glad she had offered the girl a seat. It seemed like she
really needed a friend.

God created every single person on this earth. He loves each
of them. He wants us to show that special love by giving
dignity and respect to all people. It is important to welcome
everyone, to show kindness, and to treat them as people who
are cherished by God.

Who can you be welcoming to this week?

Secret

"The time is coming when everything that is covered up will be revealed, and all that is secret will be made known to all."

LUKE 12:2 NLT

Addison was so excited to go to the science museum. There was a huge play area designed to be like outer space. It had slides. It had glow-in-the-dark areas. It had a rock wall and a large rope web to climb. She was extra thankful to go with her cousin Derek who had been there before. When he played there, he had found several secret areas with fun video games inside. Addison enjoyed the benefit of having a cousin who knew where to go.

Who knows all the secrets to the world's problems? God does. He is full of wisdom and knowledge. There is no secret you can keep from God. This shouldn't make you feel ashamed, or like you are constantly being watched by someone who is waiting to get you into trouble. Instead, it should make you feel safe. His love never changes, and he knows all of your secrets.

What secrets do you want to know about God?

Present

"Anyone who wants to serve me must follow me, because my servants must be where I am. And the Father will honor anyone who serves me."

JOHN 12:26 NLT

Everly listened intently in Sunday school. When it was over, she burst outside to play with her friends. While she was in class, she thought about God, but to be honest, the rest of the week, he never crossed her mind. Everly wanted to have a relationship with God, and she knew that meant more than a short teaching session on Sundays. She knew she would need to spend time with God every day.

You can't follow Jesus without being close to him. Just like any relationship, the more time you spend together, the more you get to know a person. It might seem weird to pray at first, but the more you do it, the more natural it feels. The more you read your Bible and sing worship songs to him, the closer you will feel to God. Ask him to teach you about who he is.

How is God present in your life?

Fullness

We pray that you would walk in the ways of true righteousness, pleasing God in every good thing you do. Then you'll become fruit-bearing branches, yielding to his life, and maturing in the rich experience of knowing God in his fullness!

COLOSSIANS 1:10 TPT

Quinn loved going to her grandma's house. Her grandma was always baking something. This time it was her famous oatmeal cookies. Quinn asked for one and then another. Every time she skipped past the kitchen and asked for one, her grandma gave it to her. At home, her mom would have stopped her at two cookies. With Grandma, she knew she would be spoiled.

You can always ask God to teach you more about him. He will always say yes. He wants you to know the fullness of who he is, so he won't hold back from you. He wants you to know all of him. Don't be okay with experiencing just a little bit of who God is and what he wants for you. Keep asking and keep seeking. He will never run out or get tired of you.

What are you asking God to show you today?

Passion

Be enthusiastic to serve the Lord, keeping your passion toward him boiling hot! Radiate with the glow of the Holy Spirit and let him fill you with excitement as you serve him.

ROMANS 12:11 TPT

Alice's mom had told her that as soon as her room was clean, she could play outside. Alice went to her room and slowly began to put things away. She dragged her feet. She read a chapter out of a book. She decided to pull all her clothes out and organize them in a new way. Her room wasn't very dirty. She just didn't feel like cleaning it. All of her distractions made the task take double the time. When she finally finished, it was too dark to go outside.

When we aren't excited about something, it can be hard to get ourselves to do it. It takes all of our energy to get motivated. Serving God shouldn't be like that. He doesn't want you to feel like he is another task to check off a list. He wants you to have passion for him. He wants you to know how wonderful serving him is. Ask God to change your heart and give you passion to serve him.

How can you increase your passion for God?

Unity

If so, make me very happy by having the same thoughts,
sharing the same love, and having one mind and purpose.

PHILIPPIANS 2:2 ICB

Ruby snatched the remote from her brother Jackson.
They were arguing over which show to watch on Saturday
morning. Their arguing had gotten louder and louder,
eventually waking up their parents. Their mom came
downstairs and told them since they fought about it, there
would be no TV for anyone. Ruby instantly felt regret. She
knew if she had just agreed with her brother, they would be
watching TV together. Instead, no one got to watch it.

To be unified means to be joined together having the same
goal. Ruby was not unified with her brother, and they did
not get to do what they wanted. God asks for his church to
be unified. It brings him great joy when his children work
together toward the cause of bringing him glory.

How can you live in unity with your family this week?

Valued

When you do things, do not let selfishness or pride be
your guide. Instead, be humble and give more honor
to others than to yourselves.

PHILIPPIANS 2:3 NCV

Brooklyn had just moved to Stansfield. It was hard to meet
people out on the farm, and she was nervous about her first
day of school. She walked into her homeroom and looked
around at all the kids laughing and chatting. In her brief
hesitation, she noticed a girl waving at her. She walked
toward her, and the girl told her the desk next to her was
empty. They begin to chat about Brooklyn's life, and she
felt her nervousness ease up a bit. The girl made her feel
welcome which gave her confidence.

You have the power to give others the gift of feeling like they
are valued. How you speak to others, the things you do, even
the reactions and faces you make all have power to make
them feel accepted. Giving people value honors God.

How can you show someone their value?

STRONG

I pray that from his glorious, unlimited resources he will empower you with inner strength through his Spirit.

EPHESIANS 3:16 NLT

Kinsley's dad was a pastor who went to the hospital every week to visit with those who were sick. Sometimes she went along with him and delivered baked goods that she had made or pictures she had drawn. After a visit, Kinsley and her dad walked out of Ms. Johnson's room, and her dad commented on how strong she was. To Kinsley, Ms. Johnson had looked very old and frail. She told her dad her observation, and he smiled at her. Though Ms. Johnson's body was getting old and weak, her spirit was very strong because of her faith in Jesus.

Outer strength we can see, but inner strength is harder to spot. Sometimes you may feel like your spirit is tired or weak. You can always pray and ask God to give you his strength. It is through the Holy Spirit that he empowers us to keep going.

Can you ask God for extra strength today?

Creative

The LORD has given them special skills as engravers,
designers, embroiderers in blue, purple, and scarlet thread
on fine linen cloth, and weavers. They excel as craftsmen
and as designers.

EXODUS 35:35 NLT

Skylar had two older siblings: a brother and a sister. Her
sister was a straight-A student. Her brother was an athlete
and head of the basketball team. Both of them were skilled
at what they did, and they excelled. Skylar compared herself
to her siblings often. She didn't feel good about much of
anything that she did. She had tried a few sports, but she
preferred to just play pickup games for fun. She did well
enough in school, but she was far from straight As. She spent
most of her time comparing her skills to her siblings, so she
couldn't see how great an artist she was. All she could see
was what she was not.

God gives all sorts of skills and talents to his children. None
of them are more important than another. The gift you have
been given can be used to glorify God, so ask him to show
you how! You will be happier when you are being true to the
way that God made you.

What is your creative gift?

Courteous

Let us consider how we can stir up one another to love.
Let us help one another to do good works.

HEBREWS 10:24 NIRV

Sadie had been discussing humility and selfishness with her
mom. She had begun to see how self-focused she really was.
She was determined to change that, so she put specific effort
into noticing the needs of others. Her mom helped her out
on the first one, telling her that it would be helpful if she
unloaded the dishwasher without being asked. She did that.
Then she noticed it was courteous to pick up her laundry and
put it away. Outside the home, she noticed the kindergarteners
needed help getting from the bus stop to the school, and
a kind word to her bus driver lifted his face. The more she
thought about others, the less she thought about herself.

A simple little task is all it takes to display the love of God. It
might seem like it's not important, but all these tiny acts of
service are like big shining gems in the kingdom of God. To
be courteous means to be considerate. What small way can
you consider someone else today?

In what small way can you consider someone else?

Loved

The LORD loved your people of long ago very much. You are
their children. And he chose you above all the other nations.
His love and his promise remain with you to this very day.

DEUTERONOMY 10:15 NIRV

Allison walked with her aunt down the long hallway. She was
so excited to meet her new brother that they were adopting.
Her parents were already at the building where they would
pick him up. He was four years old, and she was happy to
have someone to play with and to share her toys with. She
knew she loved him already the minute she walked into that
room. As they shyly said hi to each other, she felt overjoyed
that she would now have a brother forever.

When you feel loved, it is only a pinprick of how much love
God has for you. He has an overflowing, expansive, never-
ending love for you. He knows all about you and loves you in
spite of your mistakes and shortcomings.

Do you KNOW how Much God Loves you?

Careful

Be very careful how you live.
Do not live like those who are not wise,
but live wisely.

EPHESIANS 5:15 NCV

Cora's dad had a saying that he always said when he dropped her off at school or sports practice, or to hang out with her friends. "UGJ!" he would call after her. One day, her friend Rachel overheard him and asked what those three letters meant. Cora smiled. "It means use good judgment. It's just a little family saying." Her dad had thought of a quick and easy way to remind her that being wise is something that kids and adults both need to exercise.

People of all ages should consider how they can live carefully in a way that honors God. We don't get to use the excuse of being young as a reason for not living with wisdom. If you feel like you don't have wisdom, ask God to guide you.

What kind of wisdom do you need from God today?

COMPELLING

It is Christ's love that fuels our passion and motivates us, because we are absolutely convinced that he has given his life for all of us. This means all died with him, so that those who live should no longer live self-absorbed lives but lives that are poured out for him—the one who died for us and now lives again.

2 CORINTHIANS 5:14-15 TPT

Peyton had her eye on a new skateboard. She did extra babysitting jobs and then saved all the birthday and Christmas money she had been given. The idea of flying down a hill on that new board motivated her to keep adding her earnings to a jar in her room. Whenever her brothers came home with chocolate bars and tiny toys from the store, she felt tempted to also get some. Then she remembered that skateboard, and it compelled her to continue saving.

Peyton had a strong desire to buy something special. The new skateboard motivated her to do certain things. Every one of us is motivated by something. The motivation is the reason we act the way we do and make the choices we make. In the same way, when we know Christ's love it should compel us to live a life that honors him.

How does God's love compel you to live?

Discerning

"I, your servant, am here among your chosen people. There are too many of them to count. So I ask that you give me wisdom. Then I can rule the people in the right way. Then I will know the difference between right and wrong. Without wisdom, it is impossible to rule this great people of yours."

1 KINGS 3:8-9 ICB

Clara was in a pickle. She had been invited to her new friend Vivian's tenth birthday party. She was really excited about it because many of her friends were invited, and it was a sleepover. However, she had forgotten that she promised her cousin that she would run a lemonade stand with her for the city-wide garage sales. She felt frustrated that the two events conflicted. When she spoke to her mom about it, she said maybe she should pray and ask God for wisdom.

God loves giving out wisdom to his kids! You are not expected to figure out all of life all by yourself. God will help you discern the right thing to do when you rely on him to be your guide.

What do you need help discerning today?

Cooperate

Each of us has one body with many parts. And the parts do not all have the same purpose. So also we are many persons. But in Christ we are one body. And each part of the body belongs to all the other parts.

ROMANS 12:4-5 NIRV

Selah had been put into a group project with Crosby, Zara, and Maddox. The four of them struggled to work together. They were frustrated, and nothing was getting done. Mr. Gregory came over to ask what was wrong. After discussing it with them, he asked, "Why is Crosby doing research when he really wants to make posters? And why did you decide that Zara should make posters when she hates drawing and wants to present?" They realized that when they handed out duties, they did not consider the talents and skills of each person in their group. Instead of each one of them doing part they liked, they were struggling in roles they disliked.

Anyone in the world who believes Jesus is the resurrected Son of God is part of the body of Christ. Each of us has a role in the body and a place where we fit and work well. Your role will not be the same as anyone else's, and that's the way it's supposed to be.

What is your Role in the body of Christ?

AUGUST

Yes, you will suffer for a short time.
But after that, God will make everything
right. He will make you strong. He will
support you and keep you from falling.
He is the God who gives all grace. He
called you to share in his glory in Christ.
That glory will continue forever.

1 PETER 5:10 ICB

Enlightened

I pray that you may understand more clearly. Then you will know the hope God has chosen you to receive. You will know that what God will give his holy people is rich and glorious.

EPHESIANS 1:18 NIRV

Suddenly it clicked like a lightbulb had been lit up in her mind. Eliza scribbled furiously on her paper, working out the math problem. She had been staring at question number twelve for the past half hour, trying to remember the formula. She looked back through her notes, noticed the method she needed to use, and it all came rushing back to her. She had unlocked the key to understanding.

There will often be things you don't understand. When solving a problem, you can read the question again, ask for help, or try to look at it in a new way. You can take a similar approach in your walk with God. Read the Bible, ask for understanding, and pray about it. Then you will be enlightened by the Holy Spirit, so you will grasp more truth about who God is.

How has God enlightened you lately?

Flexible

When I am with those who are weak, I share their weakness, for I want to bring the weak to Christ. Yes, I try to find common ground with everyone, doing everything I can to save some.

1 CORINTHIANS 9:22 NLT

Rose was sleeping over at her best friend's house. Someone had the idea to tell scary stories as they fell asleep. Another girl went first, and as she told her tale, Rose noticed her friend, Ivy, looking uncomfortable. It occurred to her that not everyone likes scary stories, so she suggested they play a different game. Ivy's face relaxed; she seemed far more comfortable with the switch.

To be a good friend, you need to pay attention to the needs of others. You can do this by thinking about how they may be feeling. Ask yourself what would make them feel cared for? Each of us has weaknesses and strengths. Find ways you can be flexible in order to honor the needs of others.

How can you show flexibility this week?

Favor

A man of kindness attracts favor,
while a cruel man attracts nothing but trouble.

PROVERBS 11:17 TPT

Reagan had the nicest bus driver. She had known her since she was a little girl. Even though Ms. Pam didn't have a fancy job, she cared deeply for the kids that rode on her bus. She was kind, always noticed if someone had a bad day, and seemed to enjoy her job. She played fun music and remembered all the kids' birthdays. She never complained and was quick to point out things that she was grateful for along the ride. Reagan was sad that this was her last year on the bus. With her kindness, Ms. Pam had greatly influenced Reagan's life.

To be kind is an attractive quality. It always pays to be kind to others. Sometimes others will notice, but more importantly, God always does. He will have favor on you, which means at some point he will reward you for how you act toward others.

Who could you show kindness to today?

Blessed

"Blessed are those who trust in the LORD
and have made the LORD their hope and confidence."

JEREMIAH 17:7 NLT

It was Sunday morning, and Josie was walking out of church when someone told her to be blessed. She didn't know what it really meant. If it meant that everything would be perfect, she certainly did not feel blessed lately. She knew that her family was struggling with money, and things did not seem great.

When you hear the word blessed, what do you think of? Do you think of having lots of money, fun toys, or a nice big house? Maybe you think of everything being easy and going exactly as you planned. Being blessed doesn't mean having many material possessions or a perfect life. It means that you have favor as a chosen child of God. You are blessed because of what God has done for you and because of who he is.

How are you blessed?

Riches

Keep your lives free from the love of money, and be satisfied
with what you have. God has said, "I will never leave you;
I will never abandon you."

HEBREWS 13:5 NCV

Cecilia had just started a babysitting business. She had three
regular clients, so for the first time she was actually making
her own money. She enjoyed buying milkshakes at the coffee
shop, going to the mall with her friends for new clothes,
and saving up for a new bike. She thought that being able to
have all these things would satisfy her, but she found herself
constantly wanting more.

Money will never satisfy you. You can be the richest person
on the face of the earth but having all that money will never
make you truly happy. You might have a fleeting moment of
happiness, but it will not be lasting joy. Being content with
what you have means you find joy in the Lord whether you
are rich or poor. True happiness is found in him alone.

What Riches Make you happy?

Receive

Everything God created is good.
You shouldn't turn anything down.
Instead, you should thank God for it.

1 TIMOTHY 4:4 NIRV

Mina was so frustrated. This week she was supposed to go to summer camp. She had been looking forward to having s'mores with her friends and going down the giant slide into the lake. Instead, she was at home sick. She had a slight fever earlier in the week that prevented her from going, but she was starting to feel better. Suddenly, she heard a knock at the door. It was her grandma! If she had gone to camp, she would have missed her grandma's visit. Little did Mina know, this would be the last visit she would have with her grandma.

Sometimes we don't understand why things happen, like why we would get sick and miss summer camp, but God knows everything. In difficult times we have to trust that he is good and receive his gifts with faith and confidence.

What will you Receive fRoM God today?

Loyal

He will kill me. I have no hope.
But I still will defend my ways to his face.

JOB 13:15 ICB

Kaylee grabbed her rollerblades and headed out the door to go skating with her friends. She was strapping them on when she saw her neighbor, Juniper, sitting outside. Juniper looked so sad. Kaylee knew that Juniper's dad had just left them, and Juniper missed him a lot. Instead of going skating, Kaylee went over and sat with Juniper. She let her talk and cry about all the things she was feeling. Juniper needed someone to be there for her when she was sad.

To be loyal means you are faithful to someone no matter what. It means you stand with someone even when it would be more comfortable or easy to be somewhere else. One way to be loyal to others is to be with them when they are sad. People often need a listening ear when they are having a hard time. It would be far more fun to go play but loyalty means putting others' needs in front of your own.

How can you pRactice being a Loyal fRiend today?

ALL

"When you look for me with all your heart,
you will find me."

JEREMIAH 29:13 NIRV

Oakley had been asked by her mom to help her brother
clean the living room. She started to help but quickly became
distracted. Under the cushions she had found some markers.
She started doodling on a sheet of paper. Her brother was
busy putting toys in a basket, and he asked Oakley to put
the pillows on the couch. She kept doodling and didn't
even notice him do the task himself. She wasn't focused on
helping, so she wasn't very much help.

To be halfhearted is to only give a bit of your attention or
effort to something. God doesn't want us to be that way in
our search for him. He doesn't want our leftover time or our
final moments of energy. He wants our best, our all, just like
he gives to us.

How can you give God your all?

Gain

We have small troubles for a while now, but they are helping us gain an eternal glory that is much greater than the troubles.

2 CORINTHIANS 4:17 NCV

Brianna really enjoyed working with her dad in their garden. It was harvest time. They walked the rows with a basket, filling it with delicious vegetables. As Brianna picked another ripe tomato, she had a hard time remembering back to the spring and all the work they had put into the garden. She knew at times she had felt annoyed with how many weeds she had to pull and all the daily watering, but now that her basket was overflowing, those problems seemed far away.

You will have days when life feels hard or even just boring. The Bible promises us that one day we will trade in all of our troubles for the joy found in eternity with Jesus. Just like all the hard work Brianna put into her garden, the troubles you face now are helping you to one day gain blessings in heaven.

Do your troubles look small when you think about the promise of living with Jesus one day?

Radiant

His teachings make us joyful and radiate his light; his precepts are so pure! His commands, how they challenge us to keep close to his heart! The revelation-light of his word makes my spirit shine radiant.

PSALM 19:8 TPT

Destiny went to a baby shower with her mom. It was a beautiful day, and all the women had gathered in the garden with gifts and brunch for the new mom. Destiny watched the new mom with a flower crown perched on her head. Her hair was spread around her shoulders, and she looked so happy. She lightly touched her belly when people talked about her coming baby boy and glowed with delight when they imagined what he might look like. She was full of joy at the love everyone was sharing in this new life, and it showed on her radiant face.

Joy and happiness have a way of showing on our faces. Because of what God has done for us, we can be radiant. He is a good God who is so generous, loving, and kind. If you don't feel full of joy, ask God to help you.

How Radiant do you feel today?

COMPLEX

Thank you for making me so wonderfully complex!
Your workmanship is marvelous—how well I know it.

PSALM 139:14 NLT

Stella was having a hard time with math. She tried to study
more, make notecards full of formulas, and spend extra
time in the math lab. Yet no matter how hard she tried, she
couldn't get it. She would receive her assignments with low
grades and then think about how much of a loser she was.
She thought a lot of negative things about herself, and she
felt like such a failure.

Have you ever been overcome by negative thoughts about
yourself? Sometimes they feel like an attack, and other times
they sneak in like the fog. Those lies are usually from the
enemy. Never forget that you are a wonderfully complex
person, created in the image of God. He took so much care
and detail in making you, and he loves you very much.

Can you see God's marvelous work in your life?

Restored

As we wait, we trust in God's royal proclamation to be fulfilled.
There are coming heavens new in quality, and an earth new in
quality, where righteousness will be fully at home.

2 PETER 3:13 TPT

Taylor's mom owned a restoration company. She would go
to yard sales and find used pieces of furniture—old with
chipped paint and wobbly legs—for a good price. Then she
would take the piece home, paint it, and fix the leg, so she
could resell it. Taylor's mom often said that the furniture
she found had "good bones," so they were worth restoring.
People loved her pieces, and she had a lot of customers who
would prefer her restored furniture to new furniture.

Just as Taylor's mom restored furniture to be better than new,
one day Jesus will come back and make everything better. He
has promised to restore the earth to how he wanted it to be
in the first place—a perfect earth with no problems and no
effects of sin. There will be no pollution, no disease, and no
more harmful weather patterns. Everything will be perfect.

How much does the promise of a restored earth excite you?

SMART

Go watch the ants, you lazy person.
Watch what they do and be wise.
Ants have no commander.
They have no leader or ruler.
But they store up food in the summer.
They gather their supplies at harvest.

PROVERBS 6:6-8 ICB

Gianna knew all the ages for all the things she wanted to do. When she turned fourteen, she could get a job at the candy store. At sixteen, she could drive. She would graduate from high school at eighteen. She heard people talk about wisdom, and she always assumed there must be an age for it. Maybe at twenty-four? She thought it just came to everyone who hit the right age.

A certain age doesn't make you wise or unwise. The Bible instructs us on how to be wise. It is full of examples of how we can live smartly. If we follow the instructions in the Bible and ask for help understanding them, we can live with godly wisdom.

How smart are you living?

Restraint

If you live without restraint
and are unable to control your temper,
you're as helpless as a city with broken-down defenses,
open to attack.

PROVERBS 25:28 TPT

Bailey was ready to explode. She had worked so hard on her latest Lego creation, and when it was done, she had carefully placed it on the shelf in her room. Her sister had wandered into her room, pulled it down, and smashed it. She was so angry; she wanted to scream. Her insides felt like a boiling pot ready to spill over. She remembered her mom had taught her a few ways to calm down, so she took a deep breath and tried to get control of her anger.

The word restraint means that you control the emotions that feel like are about to overtake you. Just because you want to scream doesn't mean you should. Just because you want to eat all the cookies doesn't mean it's a good idea. Or just because you can watch TV all day long doesn't mean it's good for you. Learn to control your desires, and it will show in your life.

How can you show restraint?

Still

Surrender your anxiety.
Be still and realize that I am God.
I am God about all the nations,
and I am exalted throughout the whole earth.

PSALM 46:10 TPT

Autumn's piano recital was at five pm. She smoothed her dress and thought about getting up in front of all those people and playing her song. She had practiced all year, but somehow picturing herself alone at the piano made her stomach do flip-flops. She felt so anxious she thought she might burst into tears. She imagined that she might forget the notes to her song, or trip on her way up the stairs. Then she remembered the advice her father gave her: stop and pray when you feel anxious. She decided to do just that.

Anxiety is like playing a large game of What If. Your brain takes you down the road of what could happen and what could go wrong. Anxiety tells you everything is wrong, and nothing will ever be right. Playing this game keeps us second-guessing God and not trusting him. Get still with God and ask him to calm your anxious heart.

How can you be still before God today?

MORE

May God give you more and more grace and peace as you grow in your knowledge of God and Jesus our Lord.

2 PETER 1:2 NLT

Layla had just come home from a birthday party. She poured a bag full of candy onto the table and began to sort it out. She picked out all her favorites and marveled at the large amount of candy she had collected. Her dad walked into the room and spotted a chocolate bar he loved. When he asked for it, Layla told him no. She didn't want to share even one piece.

Do you know what it means to be stingy? It means to hold out on others, to be unwilling to share. God is not stingy. He isn't selfish, and he isn't withholding things from us. He could keep all that he has for himself, but instead he chooses to share generously with his children. He gives more than we even ask for. He gives us grace, wisdom, and unending peace. We can keep asking, and he will continue giving.

HOW CAN YOU BE MORE LIKE GOD?

Vigilant

"Be careful not to spend your time feasting, drinking, or worrying about worldly things. If you do, that day might come on you suddenly, like a trap on all people on earth. So be ready all the time. Pray that you will be strong enough to escape all these things that will happen and that you will be able to stand before the Son of Man."

LUKE 21:34-36 NCV

Charlotte was so excited for her best friend to visit. She had moved to Florida last year and her friend was coming to spend all of spring break with her. Charlotte excitedly prepared. She got out the air mattress and put sheets on it. She picked out snacks and meals with her mom. She made sure their spare bike had its tires pumped up and that both boogie boards were sitting by the door. She did all she could to make sure everything was prepared for the arrival of her friend.

When you are excited and looking forward to something, you take the time to prepare for it. You are vigilant, which means paying attention to the details of the preparations. We are asked to be vigilant as we wait for Jesus to return. We can do this by living lives that honor him.

How can you be vigilant about Jesus' Return?

TaLeNTed

He cared for them with a true heart
and led them with skillful hands.

PSALM 78:72 NLT

Mila loved her birthday. Her mom knew just how to make
her feel loved. She threw the best parties and always picked
a theme that Mila loved. She let her invite all her friends,
thought of fun games, and made beautiful decorations. She
made her favorite cake and served creative snacks. There was
a special crown that Mila got to wear all day, and she got to
pick all the meals they ate that day. Her mom was so talented
at making her feel loved on her birthday.

If Mila felt cared for by her mom, imagine how much more
God cares for you! Imagine how great he is at taking care
of you. He created you, and he knows you inside and out.
He knows exactly what you need. He has thought of all the
details that make you feel loved and special. You can trust
him to care for you with the utmost skill.

CaN you iMagiNe how Much God Loves you?

Understanding

If you are wise and understand God's ways, prove it by living an honorable life, doing good works with the humility that comes from wisdom.

JAMES 3:13 NLT

Hailey received a cardboard rocket ship for her birthday. It came with detailed instructions that told which piece attached where. She glanced through the instructions, but then decided she knew an easier way. She began to shove the pieces together every which way. The end result was not a rocket ship! She was annoyed. She also felt a little silly for not following the instructions.

It was a bit foolish for Hailey to ignore the instructions and then get annoyed when things didn't turn out right. This is how we often treat God's Word. We read it, and we see how he is telling us to live wisely. Then we decide to do things our own way. When things don't work out, we come back to God frustrated, but really, we are the ones who acted foolishly.

When you read your Bible, do you listen to what it says?

Efficient

Do you see people skilled in their work?
They will work for kings,
not for ordinary people.

PROVERBS 22:29 NCV

Jubilee had been asked to help her mom make freezer meals.
They would need the meals once the new baby came. Jubilee
thought it would be a good idea for each of them to pick
a meal and then make it all on their own, but her mom
disagreed. She suggested they could work more efficiently
if they each took one task, such as chopping vegetables or
browning the meat, and each person completed all of that
task. This approach made making the meals go far faster,
and Jubilee was thankful for the wisdom her mom showed.

Someone who is efficient does a job well and on time. They
use creativity to think of ways to do things that will be most
effective. You can honor God by doing your work in this
manner. It shows that you value what you are doing, and
you value the outcome.

How could you be more efficient?

Accepted

"The Father gives me the people who are mine.
Every one of them will come to me,
and I will always accept them."

JOHN 6:37 NCV

Mandy had lived in the same house her whole life. When she was ten, her parents needed to move to a new neighborhood. Mandy felt afraid of moving and meeting new people. When she was walking down her new block one day, there was an elderly lady sitting on the porch with a plate of cookies. A few kids ran up, got a cookie, chatted, and left. Mandy approached the lady and learned that she was like the neighborhood Grandma. Mandy visited every day after that because she felt so loved and accepted on the porch of the neighborhood Grandma.

It takes just one person to make you feel accepted in a new place. If one person can make such a difference, imagine what God is like. Any love a human displays, he shows it infinitely more. He will never reject you or turn you away.

Who makes you feel loved and accepted?

Adapt

When God's people are in need, be ready to help them.
Always be eager to practice hospitality.

ROMANS 12:13 NLT

Sue was always ready to help. It had become like second nature
to her. When she saw a piece of litter, she absentmindedly
grabbed it and threw it away. When her classmate forgot his
lunch, she was the first to volunteer to share. When her mom
came home with groceries, she bounded out, ready to carry
them in. What set Sue apart from others was she paid attention
to the needs around her and did her best to adapt her time and
energy to meet those needs.

To be adaptable means you can change how you act based on
what's going on around you. You discern the situation and
find a way to help. God asks us to always be ready to help
those who are in need. God is very clear about helping the
poor. We should partner with him in this by helping to meet
the needs of others.

How can you adapt to being more helpful?

Action

My children, we should love people not only with words and talk, but by our actions and true caring.

1 JOHN 3:18 NCV

Imani called out to her sister in the lower bunk. "Goodnight! I love you, Jade!" She then flicked off the light. Reaching over, she turned on her fan full blast then rolled over to go to sleep. Jade called out from the bottom bunk that the fan made her cold, but Imani ignored her. When Jade asked a few minutes later if they could please move it, Imani refused.

It's easy to say you love someone. It's harder to follow up those words with the actions that prove it. We can show other people love by the way we behave. It is loving to consider what others need and want. If you are always telling someone you love them but never considering their needs, your actions don't match your words.

How can you make your actions match your words?

COMFORT

All praises belong to the God and Father of our Lord Jesus Christ. For he is the Father of tender mercy and the God of endless comfort. He always comes alongside us to comfort us in every suffering so that we can come alongside those who are in any painful trial. We can bring them this same comfort that God has poured out upon us.

2 CORINTHIANS 1:3-4 TPT

Since she was a tiny girl, Binta had a golden doodle named Flash. The dog and the girl had grown up together. Flash slept on her bed, licked her tears when she was sad, and always greeted her with enthusiasm. When Flash passed away, Binta felt as if nothing could bring her comfort. Her mom noticed her sadness and prayed with her. Binta felt a wave of peace come over her. She knew that God was with her even when she was sad.

God has given us the Holy Spirit to comfort us. He has promised to be close to us when we are hurting. You might feel alone in your pain, but God is near. You can rely on him for comfort and strength.

What do you need God's comfort for today?

Discipline

Joyful are those you discipline, LORD,
those you teach with your instructions.

PSALM 94:12 NLT

Candice was not allowed to play her video game for two weeks. She and her brother had gotten into a huge fight over a game, and this was her discipline. She felt frustrated and defeated, but she knew they were right. There was a small part of her that felt a bit of relief as well. She wasn't sure she liked who she was after she played hours of video games. She knew the way she yelled at her brother was wrong. She wasn't happy about the discipline, but she knew her parents were helping her by giving her the mindset to change her life.

Discipline doesn't feel good at the time. Much like exercising, it is painful but good for you. God disciplines us because he loves us. He knows what is best for us, and he wants to guide us toward that.

What discipline have you experienced recently that has made you a better person?

Cover

Whoever wants to show love forgives a wrong.
But those who talk about it separate close friends.

PROVERBS 17:9 NIRV

Tessa sat with Nina outside of school. "I'm really upset
with Sara," Tessa sighed. "She broke my phone, and it's like
she doesn't even care." Nina said, "I thought you told her it
was no big deal." Tessa dug her toe around in the dirt. She
realized that she had made it seem to Sara that everything
was fine, but she was actually still upset. She probably should
not have told Sara things were fine if they weren't.

If you have truly forgiven someone, it's not helpful to
continue to talk about what went wrong. If you've dealt
with it, it's not right to hold it over the other person's head.
If someone has wronged you and it keeps coming up in
your thoughts, that is a sign that you haven't dealt with it.
Sometimes it's helpful to have a parent or another adult walk
you through forgiveness and help you fix what went wrong.

Is there a wrong you need to forgive today?

Excellent

He makes grass grow for the cattle
and plants for people to take care of.
That's how they get food from the earth.
There is wine to make people glad.
There is olive oil to make their skin glow.
And there is bread to make them strong.

PSALM 104:14-15 NIRV

Zella smiled as she opened her lunch box. It wasn't her birthday or a special holiday, but inside was a note from her mom attached to a chocolate bar. It was just an ordinary day, but her mom knew how to make ordinary days special. She often did things like that for others to show them how much she cared. These extra little things made Zella feel so loved.

God is the ultimate caretaker. Not only has he filled the earth with what we need, but he has gone above and beyond to bring us joy as well. Have you ever thought about why he made seashells such beautiful colors or why he paints a sunset every night? He didn't have to. He could have made these things less stunning. But God loves us so much he has peppered the world with wonderful things just to bring us joy. He is truly excellent.

What excellent thing has God done for you lately?

Responsible

"If you are faithful in little things,
you will be faithful in large ones.
But if you are dishonest in little things,
you won't be honest with greater responsibilities."

LUKE 16:10 NLT

Frannie was thrilled to be old enough to stay home alone. At first her mom would leave her for half an hour while she ran errands. Because those times went well, she let her stay home for a whole evening. Her mom explained to her that because Frannie was responsible in those short times, she trusted her to stay for longer times. Frannie had proved that she could make good choices while her mom was away.

It is a general rule in life that if you want to be trusted more, you need prove that you are trustworthy and able to handle small tasks, and that will pave a way for you to take on more responsibility. The choices you make in the small areas affect the big ones. When you are making choices, this is an important rule to remember.

What small things can you be responsible with?

Exceptional

"There are many fine women,
but you are better than all of them."

PROVERBS 31:29 NCV

Laquita looked around at the women gathered in her home. Her mother was holding a bridal shower for her sister, and most of the women in her family were there. Her grandma, who was kind and loving sat near the bride. Her aunt, who was the most generous woman she knew, had brought the celebration cake. Her older cousin Patricia, who made her laugh so hard, had decorated the room beautifully. And of course, her mom, who excelled in making all those who entered her home feel loved and welcome, was watching over the whole afternoon to make sure everything was perfect. What a legacy Laquita had!

Hopefully, you are blessed with the women in your life. Maybe you find your legacy of wonderful women in your community, with a teacher or a neighbor. Women who display the exceptional qualities of God are a treasure.

**What exceptional women
has God put in your life?**

Guidance

He shows those who are not proud how to do right.
He teaches them his ways.

PSALM 25:9 ICB

Kennedy felt trapped. She and her best friend were in the middle of a disagreement, and they couldn't find a solution. They went back and forth with tempers rising and hurtful words exchanged. Kennedy missed being happy with her friend, hanging out and laughing. Finally, Kennedy asked her dad for some advice. She told him all about the conflict. He led her to the Bible and prayed with her about the situation. He offered to hear both sides and work through the conflict. Kennedy was so thankful.

Those who are not proud know they need the guidance of God. When you are full of pride, you won't admit that you need help. To need help does not mean you are weak or bad. In fact, it's a sign of humility, a character trait that God values greatly. Asking for help shows that you are wise because you know that God is more capable than you are.

What do you Need God's guidance for Right Now?

Serenity

May the Lord himself, the Lord of peace, pour into you his peace in every circumstance and in every possible way. The Lord's tangible presence be with you all.

2 THESSALONIANS 3:16 TPT

In Sunday school, Molly's teacher asked them all to think of someone they were thankful for. Molly's mind immediately went to her parents. She was thankful for the good example they set for her. She knew how much her parents loved Jesus; it was evident in their life. She knew they faced hard times, but she also knew her parents found their peace in their faith. In so many ways, her parents had shown themselves to be the type of people she wanted to be.

Following Jesus is not a magical formula for a better life, nor is it a life where you always know what to do. It does mean, however, that you can always have peace. No matter what the circumstances, a believer can find peace by trusting in God. Serenity is another word to describe peace. You can have this because you can trust that God is in control.

How has God helped you experience serenity in your life?

SEPTEMBER

My mind and my body
may become weak.
But God is my strength.
He is mine forever.

PSALM 73:26 ICB

Citizen

You Gentiles are no longer strangers and foreigners.
You are citizens along with all of God's holy people.
You are members of God's family.

EPHESIANS 2:19 NLT

Five years ago, Joelle's uncle married a woman who was from Brazil. Joelle had so much fun learning about life in a different country. She loved listening to stories from her new aunt about how she grew up. Her aunt cooked foods Joelle had never tried and showed them traditions she had never experienced. Her aunt was proud to be a citizen of Brazil even though she lived in a different country now.

Many people love the country they are born in; they are proud citizens. It's good to like where we live, but as Christians we must remember that our ultimate home is in heaven. God has given you a temporary home somewhere on earth, but you are a citizen of heaven first.

Where are you from?

ReLax

That's where he restores and revives my life.
He opens before me the right path
and leads me along in his footsteps of righteousness
so that I can bring honor to his name.

PSALM 23:3 TPT

Jinn loves Saturdays. Every Saturday her family rested. On Friday, Jinn and her mom prepared dinner for Saturday, and they made cinnamon rolls for the morning. Then they spent the whole day doing things as a family that brought them joy: eating brunch, playing games, reading books, and taking naps. Everyone felt rested, relaxed, and ready to face the coming week.

God does not require endless work. In fact, he displayed the need to rest when he created the world and established a day of rest, or Sabbath. Relaxation is a gift from God. It comes in many shapes and sizes, from taking a nap to hiking in nature. It's really about connecting our spirit to God and slowing down.

How do you ReLax?

Success

Their purpose is to teach people
to live disciplined and successful lives,
to help them do what is right, just, and fair.

PROVERBS 1:3 NLT

Rowan loved her aunt. She wanted to be just like her when she grew up. Her aunt made people feel loved and cared for. This was her best trait. She didn't work anywhere fancy or make a ton of money, and she wasn't famous. She was very successful, though, because she was kind, honest, and respectful. These qualities made her stand out as the type of person Rowan wanted to be.

When you hear the word success, what comes to mind? Do you think of a person who has a lot of money, or who is in a powerful position at work? The world does not think of success in the same way as God does. God defines a person as successful when they do what is right, loving, and selfless.

What does success mean to you?

Reasonable

The wisdom that comes from God is first of all pure, then peaceful, gentle, and easy to please. This wisdom is always ready to help those who are troubled and to do good for others. It is always fair and honest.

JAMES 3:17 NCV

Maya didn't know what to do. The problem seemed simple enough: she needed to choose which sport she was going to play this year. Her parents had told her she could only play one sport during the school year. She was torn between volleyball and basketball. She had given it a lot of thought but still felt stuck. She had asked her coaches and friends, but their opinions didn't help. When she read James 3:17 in her morning devotional, she realized she had forgotten to start at the best place—with God.

God is full of wisdom on all matters of life. His answers are the most reasonable because he sees the whole picture. It takes practice to go to him first with your problems. It's not bad to seek wisdom from other people, but God should be first. He will guide you with the Holy Spirit.

Do you go to God with your problems first?

TRY

Try your best to be found pure and without blame.
Be at peace with God.

2 PETER 3:14 NIRV

Umi felt discouraged. She felt like she was always doing
something wrong. She thought about how sinning seemed
to come naturally to her. She wanted to do things God's way.
When she talked to her mom about it, her mom told her that
her feelings were very normal. Though we are all born with
sin natures, when we trust in Jesus, we are born again.

We still have to choose if we are going to live in sin or live
by the Spirit. The difference is we finally have the power to
live by the Spirit. God does not require us to be perfect. He
simply asks us to try, and to keep trying. It is by the power of
his Holy Spirit that we become pure, and he is the one who
will work on our hearts.

What have you been
trying hard to do for God?

Virtue

"He did no sin.
He never lied."

1 PETER 2:22 ICB

Jamie didn't want to study for her vocabulary test, so she didn't. Instead, she goofed off and spent the evening on social media. At school the next day, she struggled through the test. She knew she had gotten many wrong answers and wished she had stayed focused on her studying. She slowly walked to the front of the room and handed her teacher her test. Her teacher told her that because of the hard work of a boy in her class who got a perfect grade, she would also get an A+. Jamie was so surprised!

Doesn't that sound crazy to you? In a similar way, we benefit from what Jesus has done for us, even though we didn't do any of the work. Jesus is perfect, sinless, virtuous. Everything he does honors God. Because of him, your sins are forgiven.

What does virtue mean to you?

WORTH

Recognize the value of every person and continually show love to every believer. Live your lives with great reverence and in holy awe of God. Honor your rulers.

1 PETER 2:17 TPT

Valentina had many friends. It wasn't because she was the smartest kid around. It wasn't because she was the head cheerleader or a star basketball player. She didn't lead any clubs or movements. Valentina was simply kind. She treated all the people around her with respect. She was helpful, and when she spoke to people, she made them feel special.

There is not one person on the face of this earth who is not worth something to God. He loves all of us; we are made in his image. It's not our job to decide who is worthy and who is not. We can be tempted to treat people differently based on a lot of different things, but we must remember that they are worthy of respect because God loves them.

Who assigns worth to people?

Stunning

In your glory and grandeur go forth in victory!
Through your faithfulness and meekness
the cause of truth and justice will stand.
Awe-inspiring miracles are accomplished by your power,
leaving everyone dazed and astonished!

PSALM 45:4 TPT

Vanessa sang along with the song at church that talked about how God was moving. She heard a sermon by her pastor who said the same thing—God is moving. Later that week, her parents said it again. She believed it, but what did it actually mean? There weren't any major miracles happening that she saw, so what could God possibly be doing?

God is not off in a corner of heaven with his back turned toward the earth. He did not create the world just to abandon it. God is always working, and his work is stunning. His amazing creation, restoring of human hearts, and healing of sicknesses all point to his awesomeness. These are just a few of the stunning things God is doing now. If we pay attention, we will see him moving in the world.

What stunning miracles have you seen lately?

Reputation

Never let loyalty and kindness leave you!
Write them deep within your heart.
Then you will find favor with both God and people,
and you will earn a good reputation.

PROVERBS 3:3-4 NLT

Luciana felt very nervous about going to junior high school. She wasn't concerned about the schoolwork since she always did fine with her grades. She was excited for the opportunity to play in the band and try out new activities. She was nervous because she had heard about how mean the eighth-grade students were. Most of them had a bad reputation. She didn't know any eighth graders, but she had heard all about them for a long time.

A reputation is the character that other people believe you have. You can have a good reputation or a bad one. It all boils down to what you are known for. Are you known for being kind, loyal, and helpful? Or do people think you are selfish, mean, and cranky? When you strive to have a good reputation, it honors God.

What would people say about your reputation?

Remember

Be careful! Watch out and don't forget the things you have seen. Don't forget them as long as you live, but teach them to your children and grandchildren.

DEUTERONOMY 4:9 NCV

Avril was furious with her sister. All they did lately was butt heads and bicker. She slammed her door after their latest argument and plopped onto her bed. As she thought about her anger, she looked up at her bulletin board and saw the painting her sister had made her. It was an excellent painting of Avril surfing, which was something she loved to do. Avril remembered how loved she felt when she received the painting. She also remembered how her sister did care for her. It motivated her to go apologize and work things out.

In the same way that Avril remembered an act of kindness from her sister, remembering all that God has done for us can be helpful. If you feel down about your relationship with God, it is time to remember what he has done in your life.

What good thing can you remember God doing for you recently?

Resilient

When troubles of any kind come your way, consider it an opportunity for great joy. For you know that when your faith is tested, your endurance has a chance to grow.

JAMES 1:2-3 NLT

Alice signed up for a week-long track and field camp with her neighbors. It seemed like a good way to get out of the house this summer and to try something new. Alice did not know how hard it would be. When she finished the first day, she went to bed very sore. On the third day of camp, she was surprised when it was easier to run the distance. She couldn't believe how much fitter she had gotten in just three days! It was encouraging to see how much strength she had gained.

To be resilient is to not give up when things get hard. Alice had to keep running and deal with her sore muscles before she gained strength. Your spiritual life will also be hard sometimes. You might get discouraged, and it would be easy to focus on the difficulties. Instead, focus on how you can learn and grow as you go through hard times.

How can you become more resilient?

Sincere

Unlike many people,
we aren't selling God's word to make money.
In fact, it is just the opposite.
Because of Christ we speak honestly before God.
We speak like people God has sent.

2 CORINTHIANS 2:17 NIRV

When Ariana's parents prayed, they often talked about all that Jesus had done for them. Ariana considered her own prayers. She realized she came to God with a long list of the things she wanted. She knew what she wanted God to do for her and give to her, but she hadn't spent much time thinking about all he had done already, or even to thank him for her blessings.

If you are following Jesus because of what you will get from him, you are following him for the wrong reasons. God is not like a genie in a lamp who will get you what you want. Those with true and sincere faith know that they have already been given the greatest gift of all—salvation. If you have been treating God like a genie, try thanking him instead.

How has God blessed you lately?

Divine

Ever since the world was created, people have seen the earth
and sky. Through everything God made, they can clearly see
his invisible qualities—his eternal power and divine nature.
So they have no excuse for not knowing God.

ROMANS 1:20 NLT

If she could, Kristi would live outside. She adored being
outdoors no matter what the weather. She loved it all—
splashing in puddles, running through fields barefoot,
hiking in the woods, sledding down snow-covered hills.
Summer vacation was the best of all because she could be
outside from the minute she woke up until her mom called
her in as the fireflies emerged. She was so thankful for
God's beautiful creation.

The Bible tells us that we can learn about God through
his creation. All the universe and every creature in it tell a
story about who he is. It shows us how wise, creative, and
powerful he is. We can understand so much about God by
paying attention to all that he has made.

Do you see the divine nature of God in the world around you?

Driven

Without faith living within us it would be impossible to
please God. For we come to God in faith knowing that
he is real and that he rewards the faith of those
who passionately seek him.

HEBREWS 11:6 TPT

Trinidad was determined to go to camp. Her older sisters
had been, but she had never been able to go. After talking to
her parents, they decided that if she kept up her grades she
could go. It was the beginning of the school year, and she
knew she could reach her goal. The idea of going down the
big slide, having water balloon fights with her friends, and
sitting around late-night campfires motivated her greatly.

Most people have something that drives them to do what they
do. For some, it is the desire for money. Others are driven by
the hope of things to come. As a believer, what's important to
God should be important to us. Our faith should motivate us.
Ask God to help align your desires with his.

What are you driven by?

Ethical

"Well, then," Jesus said, "give to Caesar what belongs to
Caesar, and give to God what belongs to God."
His reply completely amazed them.

MARK 12:17 NLT

Ashley knew her uncle had very strong opinions about the
government. He often seemed upset, and he constantly
wanted to discuss with Ashley's dad all the things he thought
the government was doing wrong. Ashley asked her dad one
day why he wasn't as involved. Her dad explained that his
citizenship was in heaven first. He knew that no matter who
their leader was, God wanted him to show respect for them.
Ashley thought her dad's approach was the better way.

God is the true King, the King above all other kings. Just
because he is our King, it doesn't mean he is okay with us
ignoring the leadership of people. The Bible tells us God puts
rulers in place and asks us to follow the laws of the land and
respect authority. This is the ethical thing to do. We can rest
in knowing that God's authority is over all.

How can you best support a government you May disagree with?

Conscientious

Don't fail to use the gift the Holy Spirit gave you… Keep on doing these things. Give them your complete attention. Then everyone will see how you are coming along.

1 TIMOTHY 4:14-15 NIRV

Angela received a paint-by-number set for Christmas. Her parents had found a computer program that would take a photograph and turn it into a paint-by-number set. Angela was excited to get started on the picture of herself with her best friend. She read the instructions carefully. She mixed the paints exactly as it said, and she took care to make sure she was painting each section the right color for the given number. There were over one hundred numbers, so she had to pay close attention in order to do it correctly. Over time, the painting began to look like the photo.

Conscientious is a big word that means to do something carefully. This requires making sure every detail is taken care of and gets the appropriate attention. This is how God wants us to be with our gifts and strengths. He wants us to pay attention to what they are and to act on them.

How can you be conscientious with your gifts?

Surrounded

The LORD your God has blessed everything you have done;
he has protected you while you traveled through this great
desert. The LORD your God has been with you for the past
forty years, and you have had everything you needed.

DEUTERONOMY 2:7 NCV

Jenny's favorite autumn activity was to have a bonfire. As the
days slowly became shorter and colder, she loved the feeling
of the warm fire on her face. Her family would roast s'mores
and share stories over the roaring glow of the flames. No
matter how dark it got, she felt so safe in the light of the fire.
Jenny thought about how God's love was similar to the fire
because it surrounded her and brought warmth and light to
her life.

A bonfire is a good reminder to us that we are never alone.
Even if you feel alone, God is with you. He surrounds you
just like the light of the fire surrounded Jenny. He desires to
light your path and make your way straight. All you need to
do is ask him.

Do you feel surrounded by God?

Certain

We are convinced that every detail of our lives is continually woven together for good, for we are his lovers who have been called to fulfill his designed purpose.

ROMANS 8:28 TPT

Amelia reached for a jacket from the coat hooks at school. She tied it around her waist and walked out the door. At the bus stop, her friend saw her. "Hey! You have my jean jacket." Amelia told her friend she was sure this was her jacket. She tried to explain to her friend that it was exactly where she had left it. Her friend didn't believe her and asked her to look at the pocket for the smiley-face patch. Amelia was frustrated but looked anyway. There was no patch. Amelia had been certain that the jacket was hers, and she had been right.

To be certain is to have confidence that you are in a position of truth. No matter what other people say, you won't change your mind. We should be certain of who Jesus is. We can be certain that he is good, and that he is the Son of God. These truths give us a firm foundation when doubts and fears come along.

What are you certain of?

Cherished

He takes care of his flock like a shepherd.
He gathers the lambs in his arms.
He carries them close to his heart.
He gently leads those that have little ones.

ISAIAH 40:11 NIRV

Wren loved visiting her grandparents' sheep farm. Her grandpa was a big, burly man with a scruffy beard and weathered hands. His looks could be deceiving though, because he was so gentle and kind to the animals and to Wren. Her grandpa paid close attention to the needs of the animals, nursing the sick ones back to health and making sure they were all are well fed. Wren's grandpa taught her so much about care and compassion, and it reminded her of the things she had heard her pastor say about God.

God is good. He is like a kind shepherd who takes care of his sheep. He knows what we need. He cherishes each one of us. He knows how to keep us safe and heal us. He promises to lead us through life and not let us stray.

When do you feel the most cherished by God?

Accountability

Confess your sins to each other and pray for each other so
that you may be healed. The earnest prayer of a righteous
person has great power and produces wonderful results.

JAMES 5:16 NLT

If there was one thing Kylie hated, it was being wrong. She
felt nervous about getting into trouble with her teachers,
her friends, or her parents. This made her constantly lie to
make things seem better than they were. Her parents knew
this and talked to her about James 5:16. They explained that
though it was hard, she would feel so much better if she
told the truth all the time, and not just when it suited her.
It would be hard but necessary for that peaceful feeling she
wanted.

To be accountable for something means to be responsible
for it. When it comes to sin, accountability means we are
honest about what we have done. We confess our sin instead
of sweeping things under the rug and acting like they
didn't happen. God wants us to be free from sin and being
accountable helps lead us to that place.

Who are you accountable to?

Ask

"Ask, and God will give to you. Search, and you will find.
Knock, and the door will open for you."

MATTHEW 7:7 NCV

Louisa felt so nervous about her speech. She was running for
class president, and she had to speak in front of the whole
school. She practiced it and knew it very well, but all those
people made her nervous. As she read through her speech
again, she remembered she could ask God for help. When she
prayed, she felt a wave of peace wash over her. She knew that
God would be with her through this nerve-wracking time.

Asking God for what we need is an important habit to
develop. When we ask God for things, it's like we take it from
our hands and place it into his. Then we no longer need to
worry about it. He is big enough to handle all our needs.

What are you asking God for today?

Respect

Lord, teach me what you want me to do.
And I will live by your truth.
Teach me to respect you completely.

PSALM 86:11 ICB

Vida's classmates were all giving presentations. Vida loved
her project and couldn't wait to do her presentation, but she
didn't care much about anyone else's. She doodled on some
paper for the first one. Then she passed notes to her friends
for the next two. When she began to whisper with the
person behind her, the teacher caught her eye and gave her a
warning look. Vida realized that wasn't being very respectful.
She wanted them to hear her awesome presentation, so she
should show them the same respect.

You've probably been taught to give other people the same
respect you would like to receive in return. How should we
respect God? The more you get to know him, the more you
will find him worthy of your respect and praise. He is holy
and perfect, and he deserves all your worship.

How can you show respect to God?

Alive

"Just as the Father raises the dead and gives them life,
so also the Son gives life to those he wants to."

JOHN 5:21 NCV

Millie thought back on her week. She had fought with her
brother, lied to her parents about her homework, stolen her
sister's cookies, and said unkind things to the neighbor boy.
She sighed. It was easy to make a mental list of all the things
she had done wrong even in a short week. She sat down to
pray and ask for forgiveness. She was so thankful that she
didn't need to keep a list. Jesus promised to forgive her for
every single sin.

Without Jesus's sacrifice, you would be responsible for every
sin you've ever committed. Yet because of Jesus, every little
thing you have done wrong is forgiven. You are set free from
the burden of all of your wrongs, and you're invited to live
free and alive. Christians refer to this as being dead in sin
but alive in Christ.

How spiritually alive are you right now?

Filled

I pray that the God who gives hope will fill you
with much joy and peace while you trust in him.

ROMANS 15:13 NCV

Jayla was celebrating her tenth birthday. Her mom had made
the biggest strawberry lemonade cake she had ever seen. It
was her favorite. The number ten candle stood beautifully
atop the cake, and her friends and family were gathered,
singing the birthday song. When she blew out the candle,
her mom began to cut the cake. She cut a tiny piece and
handed it to Jayla. Jayla looked at her mom a bit shocked.
Her mom laughed, scooting the tiny piece aside and
replacing it with a larger slice.

God isn't handing out tiny slivers of joy. He isn't holding
back and conserving because there isn't enough. He wants
you to be full of joy. He wants you to overflow with all the
good things he has to offer.

How can you be filled with joy and peace?

Acknowledged

"What if someone says in front of others that they know me?
I will also say in front of my Father who is in heaven
that I know them."

MATTHEW 10:32 NIRV

Daphne's older sister performed in plays at her college. She
had the lead role and sung her heart out in the musical they
were putting on. On Monday at school many of Daphne's
friends were talking about the performance and how good it
was. They talked about how talented her sister was and that
she did an excellent job. Daphne felt so proud of her sister,
and she was thrilled to tell others that they were sisters.

To acknowledge means to recognize. When you
acknowledge Jesus, you tell others that you know who he
is. You tell them that you believe he is the Son of God.
Sometimes it can feel scary to tell others about Jesus
especially if they disagree. But Jesus will give you the courage
you need when you need it.

Have you acknowledged Jesus lately?

Confirmed

This is no empty hope, for God himself is the one who
has prepared us for this wonderful destiny. And to
confirm this promise, he has given us the Holy Spirit,
like an engagement ring, as a guarantee.

2 CORINTHIANS 5:5 TPT

Not once in her whole life had Eloise known her mom to lie.
When her mom said she would do something, she followed
through with it even when it was hard. This helped Eloise
know that she would keep her word. Eloise's mom had said
she could have ice cream after dinner, and Eloise looked
forward to her evening treat. Her mom was a trustworthy
person. Eloise knew God was even more trustworthy. She
felt safe knowing this.

God's Word is full of his promises. But why can we be sure
he will keep his promises? Because he is faithful; he cannot
be unfaithful. He promised to send the Holy Spirit, and
he did. The Holy Spirit confirms the promises of God. He
teaches us, guides us, and comforts us.

How can you be sure of your destiny?

Witness

You have heard me teach things that have been confirmed by many reliable witnesses. Now teach these truths to other trustworthy people who will be able to pass them on to others.

2 TIMOTHY 2:2 NLT

Keely was walking home from school past Main Street. There was a large gathering of people, so she stopped to see what was going on. It turned out a company was filming a movie in her town, and her favorite actor was the star! As he walked back to his trailer, he said, "Hi!" and spoke with her and the other people. When Keely got home, she told her brother, but he didn't believe her. It wasn't until the next day at school when everyone else was talking about it that he finally changed his mind.

If you see something happen, you are called a witness. When more than one person sees it happen, then it becomes more believable. Other people confirming details help us to know if a story is true or not.

How are you a witness for Jesus?

ENCOURAGE

When we get together, I want to encourage you in your faith,
but I also want to be encouraged by yours.

ROMANS 1:12 NLT

Kamala invited her friend Ruth to youth group. She
described all the reasons she loved going. It was a place that
made her feel at home. People welcomed each other and
quickly became friends. They studied the Bible and prayed
for one another, which left Kamala feeling comforted and
strengthened. They shared about their week and encouraged
each other. Ruth thought it sounded like a great place to be.

God created us to live in community with one another. We
need others in order to be encouraged. We were not made to
live all on our own. We can encourage others by praying for
them, saying kind things, and reminding them of the truth
in God's Word.

How can you encourage someone this week?

Active

God's word is alive and working and is sharper than a
double-edged sword. It cuts all the way into us, where the
soul and the spirit are joined, to the center of our joints and
bones. And it judges the thoughts and feelings in our hearts.

HEBREWS 4:12 NCV

Simone admitted to her mentor that she found the Bible
boring. She had stopped reading it because her mind always
seemed to drift. Her mentor understood and asked to pray for
her. She prayed that the Bible would encourage Simone and
come alive to her. Then the mentor reminded her that Bible
reading isn't just a chore to mark off; it is good for our lives.

The Bible is not a dusty, ancient book. Unlike all other books
that talk about people in ancient times, this one is alive. It
can speak truth to your heart and bring encouragement
to your soul. It can judge your feelings and your thoughts.
Reading God's Word can change your life.

How is God's Word active in your life?

Cheerful

Let the message about Christ live among you like a rich treasure. Teach and correct one another wisely. Teach one another by singing psalms and hymns and songs from the Spirit. Sing to God with thanks in your hearts.

COLOSSIANS 3:16 NIRV

Naomi loved being around her Aunt Kelli. She was her favorite person. She loved painting with her, going on walks, and talking about everything. Aunt Kelli made her feel special and had a smile that would light up a room. She never made Naomi feel like a dumb little kid but took a real interest in her life. She was like a personal cheerleader. Just thinking about Aunt Kelli coming to visit filled Naomi with great joy.

Just like Naomi received joy when she was with her aunt, your relationship with Jesus should bring you joy. Following Jesus is not meant to be a chore, a burden, or ever, ever boring! He wants you to know the joy that comes with all he has to offer.

How does knowing God cheer you up?

OCTOBER

I can do all this
by the power of Christ.
He gives me strength.

PHILIPPIANS 4:13 NIRV

Sharpen

As iron sharpens iron,
so people can improve each other.

PROVERBS 27:17 NCV

Kenna had a hard time memorizing things. For Sunday school, Mr. Greg had asked the whole class to memorize a psalm. Kenna was struggling. Then she remembered that her friend Ann memorized a lot of things for school and was very good at it. She asked Ann if she would teach her some tricks. Ann was more than willing to help, and Kenna was thankful for her friend.

To sharpen one another as the verse says means to make one another better. God gets the glory when we use our gifts to help each other. It pleases him greatly to see his children working together.

Which of your friends helps sharpen you?

Forgiveness

Higher than the highest heavens—that's how high your
tender mercy extends! Greater than the grandeur of heaven
above is the greatness of your loyal love, towering over all
who fear you and bow down before you! Farther than
from a sunrise to a sunset—that's how far
you've removed our guilt from us.

PSALM 103:11-12 TPT

Roselyn had gotten into a big argument with her sister. She
had said some very unkind things, and her sister had lashed
back. Later that day, both girls apologized, but Roselyn
couldn't seem to forget the words her sister had said. She
prayed for healing from the unkind words, for healing for
her sister, and she marveled at how God forgives and wipes
her sins away. She was very thankful.

Jesus forgives our sins. When he does, he says that they
are as far as the east is from the west—that's a very large
distance! Some could argue it's an infinite amount. The point
is to let you know it is all taken care of. We are not God, so
it's harder for us to forget. Ask God to forgive you and heal
you from the damage sin has done in your life.

What do you need forgiveness for today?

TOLERANT

Don't you see how wonderfully kind, tolerant, and patient God is with you? Does this mean nothing to you? Can't you see that his kindness is intended to turn you from your sin?

ROMANS 2:4 NLT

Dani was the oldest of five kids. She was eleven, and she knew she had earned the trust of her parents. Because of this, she got to do things her siblings did not get to do. She was able to stay up later, stay home alone, and walk to the library and the coffee shop in town. It had taken time to earn her parents' trust, and she wanted to respect their rules. She knew if she took advantage of the privileges she was given, they would probably be taken away.

God promises to forgive us of all our sins. Just because we know he will, doesn't mean we can do whatever we want. He forgives us out of his great love and kindness towards us, but he does not tolerate continued sin. His kindness should motivate us to want to do the things that he asks of us.

How tolerant are you when others sin against you?

INNOCENT

Be wise as to what is good and innocent as to what is evil.

ROMANS 16:19 NLT

Nala sat with her family around the bonfire in their backyard. The cold October air was making her shiver. She inched her chair closer to the fire. As the night went on, she kept moving a little closer. Her dad warned her that if she got too close, she would probably get burned. Nala felt so cold she didn't care. She plopped her chair within an inch of the fire. A few seconds later, a spark popped out and landed on her arm. It hurt! She wished she had listened to her father.

Sometimes we think we can inch as close to sin as possible and not get hurt. When we think we know best, and we ignore the warnings from others, there's a good chance we will face unpleasant consequences. Romans tell us to be innocent of evil, which is not easy. God asks us to stay as far away from sin as possible. We are best to listen to his wise advice.

How can you stay far away from sin?

Insightful

Help each other with your troubles.
When you do this, you truly obey the law of Christ.

GALATIANS 6:2 ICB

Jocelyn earned the nickname "big helper" when she was just a little girl. She helped her dad with projects around the house. She helped her mom with chores. She was the first one to run out and grab the groceries from the car and the last one in a store because she was holding the door open for someone. She encouraged others with her words, and she liked to help make meals to take to people who were sick. Jocelyn knew her nickname would never fade because there would always be ways to help others.

You don't have to have a nickname in order to start finding ways to be helpful. Look for opportunities—be insightful. It takes insight to know how to help someone. One person might need a hug or a compliment while someone else would benefit from a meal or help with their kids. God will give you wisdom on how to be the best help.

How can you help someone else this week?

Approval

As soon as Jesus was baptized, he came up out of the water. Then heaven opened, and he saw God's Spirit coming down on him like a dove. And a voice from heaven said, "This is my Son, whom I love, and I am very pleased with him."

MATTHEW 3:16-17 NCV

Ariel had a huge science fair project due. She had worked for three months researching and performing all the experiments it took to get her results. Her project was about bacteria, and she was very excited to present it to everyone who attended the science fair. She noticed the judges and her teacher in the crowd, but her dad stood out the most. She saw his smiling face which told her how proud he was of her. After the presentation, he gave her a big hug and used those exact words. She loved feeling the approval of her father.

Jesus is God's Son, and he approved of everything he did on earth. He was proud of Jesus, and in this section of Matthew, he told him exactly that. One of the reasons Jesus died on the cross was so that we could also have God's approval. Thank Jesus for his sacrifice for you.

Do you feel like God approves of you?

Justice

Your goodness is as high as the mountains.
Your justice is as deep as the great ocean.
LORD, you protect both people and animals.

PSALM 36:6 NCV

Dani's whole class watched the news together in the mornings. Her teacher called it "current events." Some of the reports interested her, but most of them made her sad. She didn't understand how so many bad things could be happening in the world. At lunch, her friend noticed how stressed she seemed. When Dani told her how she felt about the current events, her friend agreed with her, and suggested they pray. They asked God to bring his justice to the world.

To do justice is to do what is fair and right. God is just. He always does the right thing, and he always acts fairly. It's easy to look around and find things that are unjust, and that can be discouraging or scary. We have to remember that God has not forgotten anything, and we can trust him to right all the wrongs.

What part can you play in bringing justice to the world?

Hardworking

The plans of people who work hard succeed.
You can be just as sure that those in a hurry
will become poor.

PROVERBS 21:5 NIRV

Marigold's chore was to wash the pots and pans by hand every night. Some nights it wasn't so bad; there were only a couple of pots. Other nights, the dishes seemed endless. Marigold was tired this evening and did not feel like doing her chore. She thought if she just rinsed the pans off it would be okay. Later that evening her mom came into her room because she had noticed the pans still felt dirty. She explained to Marigold that cutting corners in her work only meant that she would have to go back and do it again. It would have been better for Marigold to do the job right the first time.

Sometimes we think that the easier route is the one that will work best. Most of the time, however, hard work is what is required to get things done, and there is always a reward in a job well done.

Are you willing to work hard?

Engaging

God did listen!
He paid attention to my prayer.

PSALM 66:19 NLT

Celia knew her family was in a busy season. Both her parents worked full time. All of her siblings were in school, and each had their own after-school activities. Taking on the care of her grandparents also took up a lot of the family's time. She didn't mind all these activities, but sometimes she wished they could spend more time with just the five of them.

Seasons come and go for you and your earthly family, but God is a constant in your life. He is never too busy for you, nor does he run out of time when you need him. If you ever feel ignored or lonely, God is right there to comfort you. He listens to every word you pray. God is engaged and aware of your life.

How can you engage in your relationship with God today?

Comprehensive

Yes, God is more than ready to overwhelm you with every form of grace, so that you will have more than enough of everything—every moment and in every way. He will make you overflow with abundance in every good thing you do.

2 CORINTHIANS 9:8 TPT

Berkley was promised that when she was twelve years old, she could learn to make her mom's famous chocolate chip cookies. When she reached the right age, her mom pulled out the classic recipe and began to explain each step. Berkley paid attention as her mom outlined the ingredients and how much she would need. There were steps that told when each ingredient went into the bowl and how to mix them properly. A specific temperature was listed for the baking, and it was necessary to leave the cookies in the oven for the right amount of time. Her mom was giving Berkley a comprehensive rundown of all things to do with her special cookies.

Comprehensive means full and complete, with all things accounted for. God wants you to fully know his love. This is a journey that will take a lifetime, but it begins today. Each day you can expand the foundation by spending time with him.

How comprehensive is God's love for you?

Approachable

O God in Zion, to you even silence is praise!
You who answers prayer,
all of humanity comes before you with their requests.

PSALM 65:1-2 TPT

Madison loved her dad; she was so proud of him. She knew she could always talk to him about anything. At school, her friends talked about how they hide things from their parents. Some said they felt afraid to talk to their parents because they didn't respond very well. Madison felt sad for them. She didn't understand what it would be like to have a dad like that. She felt blessed to have one who listens.

You can approach God. Anytime, anywhere, he is ready to listen to you. You can tell him anything, and there's no need to fear how he will respond. He knows you already, inside and out, so hiding things from him won't work anyway. He desires to know you and there is nothing that he will not forgive. He has open arms and a listening ear, so run to him today.

How do you approach God?

Committed

Commit to the LORD everything you do.
Then he will make your plans succeed.

PROVERBS 16:3 NIRV

Cheyenne handed her dad the wrench. She was helping him
fix the leak under the sink again. It had been a week, and
every other day it seemed like something else was leaking.
Cheyenne sat quietly until her dad popped his head out from
under the sink. He said, "Sometimes, you just need to ask for
help!" He asked her to hand him his phone. He was going to
call the plumber.

Committing what you do to the Lord means you welcome
him into the plan you have made. You know that he knows
what to do, and you ask for his guidance. We can trust that
God is wiser and stronger than we are. He knows exactly
what to do in all situations.

Have you committed your ways to the LORD?

Enthusiastic

Work with enthusiasm, as though you were working for the Lord rather than for people.

EPHESIANS 6:7 NLT

June loved to sing at church. It was her favorite part of the service. Some people in her church danced, some waved flags, and some prayed while the band played the songs. On this day, after the last song was played, the worship leader encouraged the group to remember that they can worship God in all that they do, and not just through worship songs. June found that interesting because she had never thought of it before. She thought that worshiping God was all about music and songs. She started to think of what ordinary tasks in her life would bring worship to God if she worked with enthusiasm.

From sunrise to sunset, your actions can be worship to God. You can honor him through your words, actions, and attitudes. You can do your chores with a good attitude and that's worship. You can be kind to someone and that's glorifying to God.

How enthusiastic are you in your work?

Admire

"The Father loves the Son and shows him everything
he is doing. In fact, the Father will show him how to do
even greater works than healing this man.
Then you will be truly astonished."

JOHN 5:20 NLT

The state women's soccer team was spending a whole week
working with Carly's junior high school team. Carly was so
excited. She looked up to the players on the university team
so much. She admired their skills and their dedication to the
sport. She knew she could learn so much from them and was
grateful to be able to go to the camp.

To admire someone means you look up to them. You respect
them and want to be like them. This might mean that you
copy what they do or shape your life to look like theirs. We
should always admire Jesus. When he walked on this earth,
his life perfectly mirrored what the Father wanted, and our
lives should reflect the same.

Who do you most admire?

CONCERN

Abandon every display of selfishness.
Possess a greater concern for what matters to
others instead of your own interests.

PHILIPPIANS 2:4 TPT

When it was time for gym, Faye and her friends rushed to the bin of balls. Not all the balls were good, so you had to act quickly if you wanted to get the best. The group argued and pushed to get the best of the volleyballs and dodgeballs. Faye kind of got pushed out of the middle, and then noticed a boy standing off to the side simply waiting. She asked if he wanted to get a good ball. He responded, "Yes, but I don't want to fight about it. I'd rather see someone else get one they want." Faye felt a bit of awe that the boy would put others' feelings above his own.

It's not easy to concern yourself with what others need. Often our own needs and wants are all we think about. It's not that our needs don't matter, but we know that God will take care of us, so we trust him.

How can you be more concerned about others?

Made

You will be faithful for all time to come.
You made the earth, and it continues to exist.

PSALM 119:90 NIRV

Ivanna saw her grandma frown. "They just don't make things like they used to!" Grandma exclaimed. Ivanna didn't know what she meant. When she asked her grandma, she gestured wildly at her refrigerator. She explained that the fridge she had before lasted for thirty years. Her new fridge was broken after five years. "The materials are cheaper, so they don't last as long."

Did you know that God made the whole world by just speaking? That's amazing! He spoke, and things came to be. And not cheap, half-hearted things either. He spoke and created a perfect world, built to last. He is so powerful that thousands of years later, it still exists.

What are you grateful for that God made?

PRaise

Praise the LORD!
Praise God in his sanctuary;
praise him in his mighty heaven!
Praise him for his mighty works;
praise his unequaled greatness.

PSALM 150:1-2 NLT

Dayana's favorite service at church was called an Encounter Service. The worship team played music, and people were free to sing, pray, read the Bible, or spend the time anyway they chose to best connect with God. Dayana dropped her backpack and sank to the floor, letting the music wash over her. She felt her body relax and calm down as she began to pray. School had been really stressing her out, and she welcomed the time set apart to praise God.

There are many things in life that can stress us out. It's important to take time to let the presence of God soothe you. When you praise him, it takes the focus off yourself and puts it back on him. Then you can enjoy his presence and listen to his voice.

What can you PRaise God foR today?

Refined

The words of the LORD are perfect.
They are like silver made pure in a clay furnace.
They are like gold made pure seven times over.

PSALM 12:6 NIRV

Penny watched with fascination as the man heated up the silver. He wore a mask and worked with special tools, carefully removing anything that he did not want in the silver. Penny's class was on a field trip to the Old Village, a place that showed how people used to live in the 1800s.

Refining is the process of making something perfect. When a silversmith heats the material up, it melts, and that causes all the imperfections to rise to the surface. Those extras are removed, leaving pure silver. This happens in our lives too. Trials, difficulties, temptations, and sin are mixed into our hearts. God's Word helps us notice them and we are refined through the fire of the Holy Spirit and work of Jesus on the cross.

Do you feel like you are being Refined?

Contribute

When you come together, each of you brings something.
You bring a hymn or a teaching or a message from God.
You bring a message in another language or explain
what was said in that language. Everything must
be done to build up the church.

1 CORINTHIANS 14:26 NIRV

Amira's favorite Sunday was the first Sunday of every month.
On that day, her church had a potluck. Everyone would
bring their favorite dish and the tables would stretch from
one end of the room to the other with a variety of foods.
Amira loved to take a little bit of each type of food to get a
rainbow of flavors. Everyone would sit down together and
eat. It was wonderful to enjoy such good food and company
at the same time.

You can compare the body of Christ to a church potluck.
Each person has something special they can contribute. If
someone doesn't contribute, then everyone else misses out.
If you choose not to use your gifts to encourage and build
up the church, the church is missing out on something
wonderful from you.

What gifts do you think God has given you to contribute?

Speak

I will tell everyone about your righteousness.
All day long I will proclaim your saving power,
though I am not skilled with words.

PSALM 71:15 NLT

Megan loved God. She knew he had saved her, he loved her,
and he was a kind and faithful Father. It was easy to chat
about these things with her church friends, but she was
nervous to share with the kids at school. She was worried
they would laugh at her, or worse, she would say something
that would make them not like God. She really didn't want to
mess it up, so she said nothing at all.

The last line of this psalm echoes the fear that other people
in the Bible have spoken about as well. Megan thought she
wasn't good with words and didn't have the skill to speak
up for God. It turns out that many people have felt like this,
even back in Bibles times! You don't need to be a gifted
speaker to bring God glory. Tell of the great things he has
done for you, and he will do the rest.

Who can you speak about God to this week?

Vital

I have depended on you since I was born.
You have been my help from the day I was born.
I will always praise you.

PSALM 71:6 ICB

Yana was confused. She had promised her little sister she would watch her favorite superhero movie with her. Her sister was obsessed; she had read all the comics and watched all the movies that came before this one. Yana, however, was not so keen and hadn't read or watched much of anything about her sister's hero. As the characters ran and flew across the screen, Yana felt like she had no idea what was going on. The backstory and details were vital to the movie making sense.

Trying to live without God is like trying to watch a superhero movie without knowing any of the vital details. It can make things really confusing. You are made in the image of God. Not only did he create you, but he is the One who knows you best. If you are trying to know who you are and where your identity is found, look to Christ.

What vital details might you be missing about God?

Invited

"I was hungry, and you gave me food. I was thirsty, and you gave me something to drink. I was alone and away from home, and you invited me into your house."

MATTHEW 25:35 NCV

Sasha was so excited to go on their family trip to the cabin. She went with her mom to the store to get all the yummy food they would need while they were there. At a stoplight on their way home, Sasha read a sign a woman was holding. It said that she needed formula, food, and diapers for her baby because she was poor. Sasha felt something inside of her tell her to give, so she asked her mom if they could. Her mom agreed they should give her some of the food and the box of diapers they had just bought. God had blessed them with enough to go on vacation, so Sasha knew she should bless others as well.

God asks us to take care of the poor. It is very important to him. With as much as he has blessed you, be generous in return. You are invited by God to work with him on his mission.

Can you accept God's invitation to be generous today?

Family

You have received the "Spirit of full acceptance," enfolding you into the family of God. And you will never feel orphaned, for as he rises up within us, our spirits join him in saying the words of tender affection, "Beloved Father!" For the Holy Spirit makes God's fatherhood real to us as he whispers into our innermost being, "You are God's beloved child!"

ROMANS 8:15-16 TPT

Shiloh had a big, loud, crazy extended family. She had four sisters and two brothers. Her grandparents lived a mile up the road. Her aunt lived in the next town and was always dropping in. Her cousins were her best friends, and her aunts and uncles were her beloved mentors. She loved her family get-togethers when they took up so much of their house and yard. There were relatives everywhere! It made her feel so loved and cared for to be surrounded by family.

A good earthly family can give us a small glimpse of being part of God's family. Not all of us have families like Shiloh's. We might feel left out of our family or misunderstood. No matter what, you will always belong to the family of God. You will always have a place there.

How does it feel to be part of God's big family?

Affirmed

Today the LORD has announced that you are his people. He has said that you are his special treasure. He promised that you would be. He has told you to keep all his commands.

DEUTERONOMY 26:18 NIRV

Amber followed her mom who was pushing the shopping cart. When they went through the aisle with the mirrors, she stopped to make funny faces at herself. Turning back around, she discovered her mom was gone! She ran to the end of the aisle and looked both ways, but there was no sign of her. Her lower lip quivered, and she felt like she might cry when suddenly she heard her name over the speaker. She made her way to the front of the store and saw her mom. Her mom told the store worker, "That's my daughter! There she is."

To affirm something means that you tell others that something is true. Amber's mom affirmed to the store worker that Amber was her daughter. God affirms that you are his daughter as well. Through the Bible, he tells you that you are loved.

Do you know you are affirmed by God?

Gratitude

Give thanks for everything to God the Father
in the name of our Lord Jesus Christ.

EPHESIANS 5:20 NLT

For the month of November, Sierra's teacher had challenged
the class to write down something they were thankful for
every single day. Sierra felt a little overwhelmed by the idea.
There were so many days! How could she think of something
for every single one of them? She sat down the first day
and thought of a simple one. The next day she thought of
something else. The day after that she considered another
idea. Surprisingly, she began to think of more than one thing
a day. Her list had doubled by the end of the time, and Sierra
noticed her heart felt lighter.

Gratitude has the power to change your life. When you begin
to find things you are grateful for, it helps you find even
more things. You realize how many gifts you have been given
by God, and it changes your heart.

What are you grateful for today?

Conduct

A voice came from heaven and said:
"You are my Son and I love you.
I am very pleased with you."

MARK 1:11 ICB

Jennifer went to the park with her little cousins. She was watching them for a bit while her aunt was at work. She pushed them on the swing, helped them across the monkey bars, and chased them around on the grass. As she gathered their water bottles to go home, a mom who was also at the park stopped her and said, "I couldn't help noticing how you take care of those two little boys. You did a great job! Your parents must be proud of how you conduct yourself with children."

Your conduct is how you act and behave. If you say that you follow Jesus, your actions should show that you follow Jesus. This means that your conduct lines up with God's Word. When Jesus walked the earth, God split open the heavens to loudly proclaim how pleased he was with him.

What is your conduct like?

Advice

Wise people can also listen and learn;
even they can find good advice in these words.

PROVERBS 1:5 NCV

Paisley sat in the passenger seat on the way home from practice. Her mom loved to listen to a certain radio program that always came on as they drove home. On the program, people could call in and talk to a person who claimed to be a love doctor. The person would give advice about relationships. Paisley's mom found the program really interesting, but Paisley found it kind of boring. She wondered what made that person even qualified to call themselves a love doctor.

It is good to ask others for wisdom, but it is also good to consider who you are getting your advice from. Some people should not be giving out advice. Turn to those who love and honor God with their lives for good advice.

Who do you ask for advice?

Devotion

Love flashes like fire,
the brightest kind of flame.
Many waters cannot quench love,
nor can rivers drown it.

SONG OF SOLOMON 8:6-7 NLT

Jacqueline hung the last poster with satisfaction. She had covered every inch of her room with posters of her favorite band. The shirt she was wearing had their faces on it. The music that was playing was theirs. When her dad walked in, he said, "My, look who is a very devoted fan!" Jacqueline didn't know what devoted meant, but if it meant that she loved this band the most, her dad was right.

A devoted person is someone who puts a lot of time, energy, and thought into an interest of theirs. God is devoted to you. His love is described as a bright flame that many waters cannot put out. The Bible tells us that God is devoted to us, but he asks that we be devoted to him alone as well.

Where does your devotion lie?

Unfailing

Your unfailing love is better than life itself;
how I praise you!
I will praise you as long as I live,
lifting up my hands to you in prayer.

PSALM 63:3- NLT

Felicity was moving to a new state. She would be leaving the house she was born and raised in and the friends she had known her whole life. Life felt very unsteady. Her parents said they would be in the city now instead of the country, and they would live in an apartment rather than a house. She knew so much would be confusing and different. She found comfort in the card her friend had written her, reminding her that though many things would change, God's love for her was unfailing and would always stay the same.

If something is unfailing, it means it never fails. It never stops, it never gives up, and it never changes. It will always succeed, and it will always win. God's love for you is all of this and more.

Have you felt God's unfailing love lately?

FIRM

Teach me to do your will,
for you are my God.
May your gracious Spirit lead me forward
on a firm footing.

PSALM 143:10 NLT

Kiara and her family were vacationing in Florida right on the ocean. Kiara was on the track team at school, and she loved to run. When her twin sister, who did not run track, challenged her to a race along the shore, she felt confident that she would win. As they took off, however, Kiara quickly realized how much harder it was to run on sand than on dry ground. She struggled to move forward, and her sister, who was prepared, quickly sprinted ahead.

Walking in the path that God has for you is like walking on solid, firm ground. Trying to follow your own direction and ideas is like running on sand—it makes everything harder! Deciding to follow the ways of the world over the ways of God is like doing your life on sinking sand; you aren't going anywhere but down. Trust God to lead you on the right path.

ARE you oN a fiRM path?

Integrity

The eyes of the LORD are everywhere.
They watch those who are evil and those who are good.

PROVERBS 15:3 NIRV

Palmer eyed the dessert table. She was in line at an after-school performance, and there was a sign that said, "Please take one." Palmer took three, because it was her favorite dessert! No one would notice, right? Wrong. She found out later that some kids didn't get any dessert, and Palmer felt guilty because she had taken so many.

To have integrity is to do the right thing even when no one is watching. Every choice we make matters. You are either becoming a person with more integrity by making small, good choices, or you are becoming a person people cannot trust. You get to choose.

What choices are you facing today that require integrity?

NOVEMBER

Because of how I have suffered for Christ, I'm glad that I'm weak. I am glad in hard times. I am glad when people say mean things about me. I am glad when things are difficult. And I am glad when people make me suffer. When I am weak, I am strong.

1 CORINTHIANS 2:10 NIRV

Joy

Those who look to him for help will be radiant with joy;
no shadow of shame will darken their faces.

PSALM 34:5 NLT

The pot on the stove was simmering. Rachel had picked a recipe out of her mother's collection and was so excited to be preparing dinner for her family. This was the first time she would be doing it all by herself. She followed all the instructions until she came across a few words she couldn't pronounce. She did not know what they meant. Confidently, she took the card to her mom. She knew her mom could help, and the meal would turn out great.

We receive joy when we ask God for help because it shows that we trust that he is big enough to handle our problems. The joy we receive comes from knowing that he is a big God, and we can be confident in his help.

What have you asked God to help you with lately?

Found

"Suppose a woman has ten silver coins and loses one.
When she finds it, she will call in her friends and neighbors
and say, 'Rejoice with me because I have found my lost coin.'
In the same way, there is joy in the presence of God's angels
when even one sinner repents."

LUKE 15:8-10 NLT

When Jamie was on vacation, she picked out a charm bracelet
as her souvenir. It had a charm on it for the tall redwood trees,
a sea lion for the ocean, and the letter J. It was perfect for her.
Unfortunately, when she woke up on Monday morning, she
could not find it. She looked everywhere, upset that she had
lost it so soon. She was just about to give up and cry when
her mom walked in the room. She handed Jamie the bracelet,
telling her she had found it after drying some clothes. Jamie
jumped up, smiling. Her bracelet wasn't lost after all!

Before we know Jesus, we are considered lost. Once we
come to know him as our Savior, we are found, and all of
heaven rejoices.

What have you found lately
that gives you a reason to rejoice?

Pardoned

Evil people should stop being evil.
They should stop thinking bad thoughts.
They should return to the Lord,
and he will have mercy on them.
They should come to our God,
because he will freely forgive them.

ISAIAH 55:7 ICB

Allie was struggling as she walked to school. She had her saggy backpack stuffed to the brim with textbooks. Across her chest she had slung her guitar case, and in her hands, she held her science fair project, her water bottle, and her breakfast burrito. She almost dropped all of it trying to open the door, but her friend Samantha saw her and ran to grab the door for her. "Can I take some of your load?" Samantha asked. "That's too much for you to carry on your own!"

Holding on to sin is like trying to balance a bunch of stuff while you open a door. There's no need to carry it when God is waiting to pardon you and take it away. He loves to show mercy, and he is always waiting for you to come to him for forgiveness.

What do you need God's pardon for today?

Prepared

Be watchful, and control yourselves completely. In this way,
put your hope in the grace that lies ahead. This grace will be
brought to you when Jesus Christ returns.

1 PETER 1:13 NIRV

Selena anxiously counted down the moments until her
mom got home from work. She loved spending time with
her mom and wanted to be with her no matter what she
was doing. Selena practically became her mom's shadow,
following her around the kitchen, laying across her mom's
bed as she talked about her day, and helping fold a load of
laundry. She felt closer to her mom because she knew where
she was an what she was doing.

The Bible promises us that one day Jesus will return. We
aren't told when this will happen just that it will happen, and
we need to be prepared. The best way to prepare for this is to
stay close to Jesus.

How can you be prepared for Jesus to return?

Relief

Hear my prayer, O LORD;
listen to my plea!
Answer me because you are faithful and righteous.

PSALM 143:1 NLT

Janis enjoyed hiking with her family. It was the one activity that all six of them could agree on. Today, her family was tackling a longer trail. They had already done four miles and she knew there were more to go. Her legs ached, and she regretted packing that extra notebook in her backpack. When everyone stopped for a snack, she asked her dad if he could carry her backpack for a little while. Her dad smiled and agreed.

What a relief that Janis had her father who could carry that weight for her! When you hand over your worries and cares to God, it's just like handing over a big backpack that is weighing you down. Your heavenly Father can handle it; he is big enough to carry everything for you while you rest.

What burdens do you need God to relieve you of right now?

Fair

If you judge someone else, you have no excuse for it.
When you judge another person, you are judging yourself.
You do the same things you blame others for doing.

ROMANS 2:20 NIRV

Robin finished washing her hands and grabbed her spot at the dinner table. Tonight, her mom had cooked her favorite meal—spaghetti and meatballs complete with a basket of buttery garlic bread. They enjoyed the meal, and Robin went in for a second helping. There was one roll left, and just as she reached to grab it her older brother swooped it up. "Hey! No fair!" she yelled at him. Her dad instructed her brother to split the piece in two after an apology.

The Bible tells us to treat others the way we want to be treated. This is being fair. It's only fair to behave the way you expect other people to behave. It doesn't make sense to be upset about someone's actions when you act the same way. Being fair can be hard, but it is what God asks us to do.

How can you treat others with fairness?

Sensible

"Teacher, which command in the law is the most important?"
Jesus answered, "'Love the Lord your God with all your heart,
all your soul, and all your mind.' This is the first and most
important command. And the second command is like the
first: 'Love your neighbor as you love yourself.'"

MATTHEW 22:36-39 NCV

Betsy went on a field trip with her class to the art museum.
She was so excited to see the new exhibit they had brought
to town with real mummies in it. It was cool to see all the
ancient artifacts up close. In the gift shop, they had tiny
replicas of one of the Egyptian queen's tombs. Betsy knew
it was the perfect souvenir. When she got to the front of the
line, there was one left. Earlier she had heard the girl behind
her telling her mom how excited she was to get one. Betsy
thought for a moment and then offered the souvenir to the
girl. The other girl's smile made it worth it.

If you don't know how to love others, think of how you
would want to be treated. It's pretty sensible, really. If you
want other people to share with you, share with them. It
takes effort, but it is not complicated.

How sensible is God's commandment to love others?

Shelter

In the depths of my heart I truly know
that you, Yahweh, have become my Shield;
you take me and surround me with yourself.
Your glory covers me continually.
You lift high my head.

PSALM 3:3 TPT

Shelly and her friends were biking to the park when it began to rain. The light drizzle felt refreshing at first, but then it really began to pour. When they heard the clap of thunder, they knew they needed to find a place to take shelter. Quickly they biked over to a small pavilion and dragged their bikes inside. They waited under the safety of the pavilion as the crazy storm passed by. The shelter kept them safe and dry until the storm passed.

God is our shelter. He is the one who keeps us safe and protected from the storms of life. When we feel like a lot of sad things are happening and we become anxious or overwhelmed, we can always count on him to provide a place to rest and feel safe.

How can God be a shelter to you today?

TENDER

The LORD is like a father to his children,
tender and compassionate to those who fear him.

PSALM 103:13 NIRV

Stephanie walked tentatively down the hospital hallway. She was on her way to meet her new baby sister. She couldn't believe the baby was finally here! When Stephanie entered the room, she saw her mom sitting in the hospital bed and her dad sitting by the window. Her dad was gently rocking the tiny baby. Stephanie watched in awe at how gentle and sweet he was, singing her back to sleep and tenderly stroking her face. If her big, strong dad could be so compassionate to a tiny baby, Stephanie imagined how God would treat her.

Since you are a child of God, he is tender and compassionate toward you. What happens to you matters to him. Remember when you approach him that he is a gentle, loving God.

How have you experienced the tenderness of God?

Treasured

People were bringing little children to Jesus. They wanted him to place his hands on them to bless them. But the disciples told them to stop. When Jesus saw this, he was angry. He said to his disciples, "Let the little children come to me. Don't keep them away. God's kingdom belongs to people like them."

MARK 10:13-14 NIV

In the eyes of Carlene, no one was cooler than her Aunt Lisa. Whenever she came to visit, Carlene knew it would be a great time. Aunt Lisa was one of those adults who actually listened, and she treated people like they were the only ones in the room. She was an artist, and Carlene loved to try out new painting methods with her. Aunt Lisa always had the best stories and great fashion advice too. Carlene felt important and loved when she was in town.

You are greatly treasured by God. That means you are of huge value and importance to him. He loves when you talk to him. He is never too busy for you. If there is someone who makes you feel loved and cared for like Aunt Lisa, just imagine how much more God treasures you.

When do you feel treasured?

Resist

Put on every piece of God's armor so you will be able to resist the enemy in the time of evil. Then after the battle you will still be standing firm.

EPHESIANS 6:13 NLT

Kisha knew the right thing to do. Hitting her brother was wrong, but sometimes he made her so angry! He would constantly pick on her until she couldn't take it anymore. At that point, she had a hard time controlling her emotions. She knew hitting wasn't the answer, but she didn't always feel like she could resist the urge.

To resist means to choose not to do or think something. It is an active choice. Did you know that God gives us everything we need to resist sin? When you are tempted to do something wrong, you must remember that you have power through the Holy Spirit in you to resist. This is the same power that raised Jesus from the dead. It cannot be beat.

What do you Need to Resist today?

Priority

Here is what people who belong to this world do. They try to satisfy what their sinful desires want to do. They long for what their sinful eyes look at. They take pride in what they have and what they do. All of this comes from the world. None of it comes from the Father. The world and its evil desires are passing away. But whoever does what God wants them to do lives forever.

1 JOHN 2:16-17 NIRV

Savannah was having a hard time in her English class. She didn't want to take the time to read the books Ms. Kennedy had picked out. She especially didn't want to write all the papers on those books once she had read them. There were so many other fun things she could be doing. When the school called, her dad sat her down to talk about the unwritten papers. He told her that, although seeing her friends and playing basketball were important, she needed to prioritize her schoolwork if she wanted to pass.

When you make something a priority in your life, it means that you put it first. If you are a believer, you should always make God your main priority. There are so many ways to put him first: pray, read the Bible, be grateful, and teach others about him.

What is your top priority?

PRovide

"Why do you worry about clothes? Look at the flowers in the
field. See how they grow. They don't work or make clothes
for themselves. But I tell you that even Solomon with his
riches was not dressed as beautifully as one of these flowers.
God clothes the grass in the field like that. The grass is living
today, but tomorrow it is thrown into the fire to be burned.
So you can be even more sure that God will clothe you.
Don't have so little faith!"

MATTHEW 6:28-30 ICB

Emily snuggled deeper into her bed. She thought about the
fact that she never had to worry about what she needed.
Each day she woke up to plenty of food. Each night she laid
in a warm bed. She had clothes, a dry house, and a way to get
to school. She never worried about any of the basic needs.
Her parents worked hard for their family, making sure the
kids were all happy and healthy.

Parents work hard to provide for their kids. Imagine how
much more God takes care of you. He has endless resources.
Humans are the most important part of his creation. If he
takes care of the birds and the trees, of course he will take
even better care of you.

What has God PRovided foR you LateLy?

Safe

The Sovereign LORD is my strength!
He makes me as surefooted as a deer,
able to tread upon the heights.

HABAKKUK 3:19 NLT

It was a beautiful day to go skating. Maxine loved rollerblading with her friends. The weather felt nice and crisp as they set out down the familiar streets. One road they always took had been under construction recently. Maxine and her friends looked ahead and saw the road was covered in gravel. They decided to take a different route because the rocks would make them fall. Good thing they had paid attention!

God is always there to keep you steady and safe. He knows the path ahead and what your days will look like. The Bible tells us that he goes before us. When you listen to God, you are trusting him to guide you through your days. Just like Maxine and her friends stayed away from the dangerous gravel, listening to God is a good idea if you want to steer clear of potential hazard areas in life.

How does following God make you feel safe?

Awake

"I say to everyone—
be awake at all times."

MARK 13:37 TPT

Martha had always wanted to see if she could stay up all night. Martha's parents agreed but said it had to be a Friday night. Then she could try to stay up all night. At first it was easy. She ate snacks and watched movies with her sister. Once the early morning hours rolled around though, Martha's eyes felt heavy. The desire to sleep was so strong! She couldn't fight it anymore. The next morning, she woke up to her parents standing over her, smiling.

When the Bible tells us to stay awake, it's not talking about pulling an all-nighter like Martha tried to do. It's about being alert to what is happening in the world around you. There is a spiritual battle, and we often cannot see it. Being awake means you are aware of temptation. If you are alert enough, you will also notice opportunities to honor God.

How can you be spiritually awake?

Confident

We are confident of all this
because of our great trust in God through Christ.

2 CORINTHIANS 3:4 NLT

Melanie had to draw a map of all the countries in the world
at school. Each week she studied a new section of the map,
drawing it over and over again. Finally, by the end of the
year, she was confident that she would pass the exam. She
knew that the work she had put into memorizing, mixed
with her love for geography, would help her ace this test.

When you are confident about something like Melanie was,
it means you are very sure. Just like Melanie was confident in
her ability to pass the geography exam, we can be confident
in God's ability to do what he says he will do. He is a faithful
God who always keeps his promises. You don't have to put
your confidence in your own strength and ability because
God is with you every step of the way.

How confident are you in God's promises?

Ambitious

We want each of you to go on with the same hard work all your lives so you will surely get what you hope for.

HEBREWS 6:11 NCV

Fiona wanted to be on the junior varsity soccer team. It was a lofty goal, but she was determined to achieve it. At practice, she enthusiastically ran her drills. She stayed late and showed up early, and she constantly asked the coach for feedback on how she could improve. She put everything she could into achieving her goal. At the tryouts for the team, all her work paid off. The coaches noticed her ambition and gave her a starting spot on the team.

A person who is ambitious wants to succeed at what they are doing. It means they are not afraid of the hard work it takes to get where they want to go. Many people think ambition mainly has to do with jobs, school, and sports, but you could also be ambitious in trying to love your friends or family well. That is ambition that will pay off with a life in eternity.

What are you ambitious about?

UNWORRIED

There is no fear in love. Instead, perfect love drives away fear.
That's because fear has to do with being punished.
The one who fears does not have perfect love.
We love because he loved us first.

1 JOHN 4:18-19 NIRV

Have you ever seen an animal camouflaged in its natural habitat? It's really quite amazing! God gave some animals the unique ability to hide from their predators. For instance, there is a butterfly that has wings that fold up to look like a dead leaf! This enables them to blend into their surroundings. Since God took care in creating the smallest of animals, how much more will he take care of you when you have concerns and fears?

God will provide the protection we need. Many of the things we fear don't have to worry us anymore because we have God. We never have to fear being alone, being rejected by God, or facing death. Jesus overcame death, and we will live forever with him.

How can you choose not to be worried?

Esteem

You should want a good name
more than you want great riches.
To be highly respected
is better than having silver or gold.

PROVERBS 22:1 NIRV

Sophia was getting ready to go into sixth grade. That meant she would be moving from elementary to junior high. Many of her friends were nervous about fitting in, but Sophia knew she would be just fine. She was already known as "Brad's little sister." Some people might have found it annoying to be labeled like that, but Sophia loved it. It meant that everyone knew Brad was her older brother, and he would be looking out for her. He was smart, kind, and strong. The teachers loved him, and he had many friends. His good name was paving a road for Sophia.

Your character and reputation are important. To be esteemed by others means that when people think of you, they think good things. Just as Brad has a good reputation at his school, you can put effort into creating the best reputation for yourself as well. You should strive to be known as a girl who loves and follows Jesus.

Who do you esteem?

WILLPOWER

"My food is to be doing the will of him who sent me and bring it to completion." As the crowds emerged from the village, Jesus said to his disciples, "Why would you say, 'The harvest is another four months away'? Look at all the people coming—now is harvest time! For their hearts are like vast fields of ripened grain—ready for a spiritual harvest."

JOHN 4:34-35 TPT

Colleen wandered through the pumpkin patch deep in thought. Her parents had given her ten dollars to spend at the market. She really wanted to buy herself a big bucket of donuts and a tall cup of cider and gulp it down all by herself. But all she could think about was her sister who was stuck at home. Her sister had gotten sick and couldn't come. She knew that her sister had been looking forward to the pumpkin patch. Maybe she could buy some donuts to share with her and a few pumpkins that she and her sister could paint at home instead. Colleen chose to do something good for her sister instead of spending all her money on herself.

Willpower is the ability to control your actions and your emotions. Every day you can choose to be selfish, only doing the things that you want to do, or you can deny yourself and find ways to bless others by putting them first.

Do you have the willpower to put others before yourself?

Righteous

May you always be filled with the fruit of your salvation—
the righteous character produced in your life
by Jesus Christ—for this will bring much glory
and praise to God.

PHILIPPIANS 1:11 NLT

Mariah stood in line at the theme park. She was patiently waiting with her parents to buy tickets. While she waited, she read different signs. One sign listed the different prices. Kids were ten dollars, adults cost twenty dollars, seniors were only fifteen dollars, but anyone who served in the military got in for free. She tugged on her dad's shirt. "Dad! It says you can get in for free!" Her dad explained that only people in the military could get that discount and he didn't qualify. No one in their family had ever served in the military.

When someone is righteous, it means that they are in right standing before God. We are made righteous because of what Jesus did on the cross. Knowing Jesus and having faith in what he did on the cross is what qualifies us. Trying to stand in God's presence without Jesus is like trying to use the military discount without being in the military.

How does it feel to be Righteous before God?

Journey

In the same way you received Jesus our Lord and Messiah by faith, continue your journey of faith, progressing further into your union with him! Your spiritual roots go deeply into his life as you are continually infused with strength, encouraged in every way. For you are established in the faith you have absorbed and enriched by your devotion to him!

COLOSSIANS 2:6-7 TPT

Diana set the book down. What a satisfying ending! Diana greatly enjoyed adventure books. She loved it when the main character went on a journey through unknown lands and faced new challenges. The suspense kept her from putting the book down, but the ending was always so satisfying.

Our relationship with God is a journey. Along the way there will be many unknowns and challenges. We may even want to quit or turn back. Following Jesus is a lifetime full of choosing him over everything else. You build your faith day by day, and moment by moment. Together, the steps of your journey will make for one epic adventure as you trust God and do what he says. Hopefully, you will never stop growing in your faith and becoming more like Christ.

What do you love about your faith journey?

Fortress

The Lord is my light and my salvation—
so why should I be afraid?
The Lord is my fortress,
protecting me from danger,
so why should I tremble?

PSALM 27:1 NLT

Kandy was putting the finishing touches on her project for history class. She had built a medieval castle out of blocks. She had learned so much during this project, like how the knights went on quests and were told to protect the kingdom from invaders. She had also learned how they had to stand up on the tall, thick walls that surround the castle to be on the lookout for invaders. These well-built walls helped the knights see for miles so they could keep the enemy out of their fortress.

Just like fortresses and medieval castles, God surrounds and protects us. He keeps us safe with a stronghold that can't be beaten. The God of the whole universe is on your side ready to protect you. There is no need to be afraid.

How is God like a fortress to you?

Thankful

No matter what happens, tell God about everything.
Ask and pray, and give thanks to him.

PHILIPPIANS 4:6 NIRV

Christina felt horrible. She was shaking under several layers of blankets because she felt cold. She hated being sick and missing school. Her throat felt raw, her head throbbed, and she couldn't breathe out of her nose. She was very crabby and annoyed by the whole situation. When she heard a little knock on the door, she peaked out from under the covers. Her mom came in holding a tray of warm chicken soup. Together they watched Christina's favorite movie while the chicken soup warmed her up from the inside. She was so thankful to have such a kind mom.

When life is hard, it can be very difficult to find things you are thankful for. Even in the worst situations, there is always something good. Learning to be thankful in hard times is not an easy task. It takes practice.

What are you thankful for today?

Reconcile

"When you are praying, and you remember that you are angry with another person about something, then forgive him. If you do this, then your Father in heaven will also forgive your sins."

MARK 11:25 ICB

When Michelle got to the park, she saw her neighbor Maddie. Immediately she wanted to run back home. Michelle felt frustrated as she remembered what happened last time she and Maddie played. There was a huge argument and both girls went home upset. She hoped Maddie hadn't see her as she turned to go, but then she heard her name. Maddie ran up to apologize for what she had said. Michelle felt her anger shrinking as the two girls discussed the argument. They talked about how each of them felt and came to a resolution.

To reconcile with someone means to restore your relationship. When you have a problem with someone, the best way to fix it is to talk through your feelings and seek forgiveness. If you hold onto anger, it will grow into bitterness and choke out your peace. When you are wrong, humbly ask for forgiveness. When you've been hurt, ask God to help you forgive.

Is there anyone you need to reconcile with?

Credit

Remember the LORD in all you do,
and he will give you success.

PROVERBS 3:6 NCV

Kayla couldn't wait to show her friends her brand new tree house. When they came over, she and her friends ran to the backyard to play. They noticed all the important details that her dad had put into it for her. She felt so proud of it, she almost said that she had built it herself. She knew that wasn't the truth. Though she had helped, her dad had done most of the building himself. It wouldn't have been fair to tell them she did it alone.

Giving someone credit for something means that you tell others the work they did. It is wrong to take ownership of things we didn't do. As Christians, we are supposed to give credit to God for everything that we do that is within his plan. It is his strength that gives us our success.

What can you give God credit for today?

Helped

Because the Sovereign LORD helps me,
I will not be disgraced.
Therefore, I have set my face like a stone,
determined to do his will.
And I know that I will not be put to shame.

ISAIAH 50:7 NLT

Kiara wanted to bake a cake for the county fair. She bought all the ingredients and picked out the recipe. She had baked many things before, but she was excited to work on this particular cake. She felt confident that it would turn out really well, partly because her Uncle Dave said he would help her. Dave owned a bakery in town, and he had been making cakes for thirteen years. She knew she could rely on his skill to help her succeed.

Kiara needed help to make her plan of baking a cake a true success story! For that reason, she turned to a professional. In the same way, if you need your car fixed, you take it to a mechanic, not a baker. You can turn to God for everything and be confident he will help you. No matter what you are going through, he is capable of helping you.

What do you need help with today?

Victorious

I trust in your love.
My heart is happy because you saved me.
I sing to the LORD
because he has taken care of me.

PSALM 13:5-6 NCV

Every year on Thanksgiving Day, Deja's family held a few friendly competitions. There was the flag football game, the three-legged race, and the tug-of-war. She loved competing against her cousins. What she really loved though, was how it felt to win. It was such a happy relief when she came out on top. She felt pride as she accepted the homemade medal her grandparents handed out, and she proudly displayed it for the rest of the weekend.

Did you know that you are victorious because of God's love? Because of what Jesus did on the cross, you are on the winning side. You win for all of eternity because of him. No matter what happens in life, you can rejoice because God has won. This victory will never change or be removed!

Have you thanked God for giving you victory lately?

Truthful

"The Spirit of truth. The world cannot accept him,
because it does not see him or know him. But you know
him, because he lives with you and he will be in you."

JOHN 14:17 NCV

Shanice sat at the kitchen table listening while the grown-ups talked. Today was Shanice's older sister's bridal shower. She was getting married in one month. Shanice smiled as she listened to her sister gush about her fiancé. She was full of kind and wonderful things to say about him. Every present she opened she talked about how much he would love it. Everything reminded her of her fiancé. From everything her sister said, Shanice felt like she knew him and felt confident he was a great guy.

This is how the Holy Spirit works. No matter what, the Holy Spirit will always remind you of the goodness of God. It can be hard sometimes to know what is true and what is not. If you allow him, the Holy Spirit will always point you to the truth. He will remind you of what the Bible says and what God has spoken to you. He will tell you of all the great things God has done and help you not to be deceived.

How can you remain in the truth?

Unselfish

"I came down from heaven to do what God wants me to do.
I did not come to do what I want to do."

JOHN 6:38 ICB

Helena loved her new ballet class. She had always wanted
to learn ballet and was excited to be under Ms. Bree as her
instructor. As Ms. Bree danced, Helena tried her best to
move just like she moved. She corrected her feet when she
was told and watched her teacher very carefully. She knew
she was learning from the best, and everything Ms. Bree did,
she copied.

Jesus did not come to earth with his own plans. The Bible
tells us he did exactly what the Father said to do. Jesus was
never selfish. He always thought about what the Father
wanted. Just as Helena learned about ballet by doing what
Ms. Bree did, you can learn about who God is by following
Jesus. If you follow his example, you will learn how to be
unselfish.

How can you live an unselfish life?

DECEMBER

Look to the LORD
and to his strength.
Always look to him.

1 CHRONICLES 16:11 NIRV

Wait

Be still in the presence of the LORD,
and wait patiently for him to act.
Don't worry about evil people
who prosper or fret about their wicked schemes.

PSALM 37:7 NLT

Jessica didn't think she could stand the anticipation any longer. Christmas was twenty-four days away! It was her favorite holiday. She loved getting out the decorations, baking cookies, watching Christmas movies, being in the Christmas play, and hearing the story of the birth of Jesus. She enjoyed picking out gifts for her siblings and wondering what could be in the boxes that had her name on it. The hardest part was waiting!

Waiting is a normal part of life. From exciting events like Christmas Day to everyday things like buying groceries, we often have to wait. We don't like to wait when it comes to God either. We expect him to fix a problem as soon as we pray about it. This isn't how he always works. God is wise, and he knows what's best for us—sometimes that means waiting.

How have you seen God's perfect timing in your waiting?

New

This means that anyone who belongs to Christ has become a new person. The old life is gone; a new life has begun!

2 CORINTHIANS 5:17 NLT

Genevieve loved drawing on the whiteboard at school. Her teacher always had a variety of colors, and she could fill the whole board with rainbows, sunshines, and girls in fancy dresses. The best part about the whiteboard was if she made a mistake or wanted to start a new drawing, she just wiped it off, and the board was clean again. It was like a brand-new canvas.

Just like Genevieve could easily wipe away all the marks and have a fresh, clean board, your soul is clean and new because of what Jesus did on the cross for you. All the mistakes and sins of your past have been wiped clean the minute you confessed. You stand before God with a new life; this is the miracle of the cross.

How does it feel to be made new?

Favorite

In Christ, there is no difference between Jew and Greek,
slave and free person, male and female.
You are all the same in Christ Jesus.

GALATIANS 3:28 NCV

It was time for Christmas break, and Adele was so excited!
She, her mom, and her dad were driving to her grandma's
house to spend time with her family. She pushed one more
of her stuffed animals into her bag and ran out the door.
She almost made it to the car before her mom stopped her.
"Adele, we don't have room for so many stuffed animals!"
She asked Adele to put a few back. How was she supposed to
leave anyone behind?

Do you have a favorite stuffed animal? Everyone has things
they prefer—food, movies, books, toys—that's totally
normal. God, however, does not play favorites. He doesn't
think men are better than women, or that a certain color
of skin is greater than another. Of all the billions of unique
people who have been on this earth, his love for each
of them has always been the same. That is a perfect and
powerful kind of love!

What are some of your favorite things?

Courage

"Do not be afraid," he said. "You are highly respected.
May peace be with you! Be strong now. Be strong."
When he spoke to me, I became stronger. I said,
"Speak, my master. You have given me strength."

DANIEL 10:19 NIRV

Melissa loved everything about the snow: everything, that
is, except driving in it. She had heard about people losing
control of their cars and getting into accidents. She had a
lot of anxiety that this would happen to her as well. Snow
was falling heavily by the time her concert was done and her
family got in the car. Seeing the worried look on her face, her
dad reassured her that he had driven in the snow for many
years—before she was even born. This put her mind at ease
because she had confidence in her dad.

When God tells us that we should be full of courage, he's
not expecting us to get there on our own. Because God is on
our side, we can be brave. He has been running things a lot
longer than we have been around, so we can be courageous.
We just have to trust in God.

How can you build courage today?

Meek

"When you give to someone in need, don't do as the hypocrites do—blowing trumpets in the synagogues and streets to call attention to their acts of charity! I tell you the truth, they have received all the reward they will ever get."

MATTHEW 6:2 NLT

Nancy felt proud of her mom. No one really mentioned it, but Nancy knew all the kind things her mother did for others. She helped as her mom made meals to take to sick people or new mothers. She saw her mom watch other people's children, so they could take a break. She watched her pick up groceries for elderly people. Her mom never bragged or talked about it much, but Nancy saw how kind her mom was to everyone she came across.

Nancy's mom was a great example of what it means to be meek. She could have let everyone around her know the kind things she did, but she didn't. She didn't search for the praise of others; she knew that God would reward her in his time.

How could you be more meek?

Perseverance

Be patient until the Lord comes. See how the farmer waits
for the land to produce its rich crop. See how patient the
farmer is for the fall and spring rains.

JAMES 5:7 NIRV

Trillin couldn't help herself: she glanced at the calendar again.
Time seemed to be going so slowly! She was still six months
away from her tenth birthday. When she turned ten, her
parents told her she could have a room all to herself. Until
then, she had to show them she was responsible by keeping
her room clean. Turning ten couldn't get here fast enough!
She was tired of cleaning up, but she wasn't going to quit.
With a little perseverance, that new bedroom would be hers!

Perseverance is the ability to keep going even when
something is difficult. When you want to give up and quit
but you don't, that means you are persevering. Sometimes
following Jesus can be the hardest thing you are doing. It's
important to be patient and not give up when things get
difficult.

How do you show perseverance?

Healing

The man jumped up and went home!
Fear swept through the crowd as they saw this happen.
And they praised God for giving humans such authority.

MATTHEW 9:7-8 NLT

Courtney sat in the waiting room at the hospital with her parents. Her brother had been in surgery for a really long time. Finally, the doctor came out and spoke with her parents. She overheard the word miracle. Her parents came over to her with big smiles on their faces. The doctor said it had been a miracle, and her brother would come through just fine. Courtney was so excited. This was exactly what she and her parents had prayed for that morning—a miracle! God heard her!

God still does miracles today. He does these miracles, big and small, to give us a glimpse of what eternity with him will be like. The sick will be healed, there will be no more tears, and no one will ever suffer again.

What healing have you prayed for?

Protection

The Lord sees all we do;
he watches over his friends day and night.
His Godly ones receive the answers they seek
whenever they cry out to him.

PSALM 34:15 TPT

Wendy finished the babysitting class easily. Now she was greatly enjoying her first real job. She watched Bobby and Nate, the little boys who lived across the street. Though it was fun, it was also hard work. She had to make sure Nate stayed away from stairs, and she had to constantly take things out of Bobby's mouth. Wendy watched diligently to make sure neither of the boys went outside alone. Keeping curious toddlers safe kept Wendy busy!

God is our caretaker. He watches over us even when we are unaware. He makes sure we are safe and that we have the things that we need. Just like Wendy watched over the boys, God is watching over you. He protects you even when you don't know that you need to be protected.

How do you feel knowing that God watches over you?

COMPASSION

If anyone sees a fellow believer in need and has the means to help him, yet shows no pity and closes his heart against him, how is it even possible that God's love lives in him?

1 JOHN 3:17 TPT

Missy reached into her backpack to grab her lunch, but she couldn't find it! She must have left it at home, and it was too late for her mom to drop it off. She didn't even have a dollar for the vending machine. As she sank into a chair trying to figure out what to do, her classmate Natasha leaned over and handed her a sandwich. Missy looked up, surprised. Natasha explained she had a huge breakfast and wouldn't be able to finish both sandwiches. Missy was so thankful that Natasha showed her such compassion.

The Bible teaches that whenever an opportunity comes, we should help others. As you grow older you will begin to see that not everyone's life is the same. Some have good jobs, others don't. Some have nice homes with all the food they need, and others struggle to get by. God wants us to be generous and compassionate.

How can you be compassionate today?

Dedicated

"The Lord searches all the earth for people
who have given themselves completely to him.
He wants to make them strong."

2 CHRONICLES 16:9 ICB

Lydia loved to play hockey. She waited all year for hockey
season. She loved the feeling of her skates cutting across the
ice, the weight of her gear, and the chill in the air. When she
wasn't playing hockey, she was watching hockey, or talking
about hockey, or planning on how she would get to play for
her favorite team. Maybe one day she would even go to
the Olympics!

When you dedicate yourself to someone or something, you
are loyal to that person or cause. God asks us to be faithful to
him. He doesn't want to be a good idea or a one-time prayer;
he wants you to follow him with your whole heart and
devote your life to him. When you follow Jesus, you say
you will love him with everything you have.

Would you say you are dedicated to God?

Belief

All the people were amazed and said,
"Perhaps this man is the Son of David!"

MATTHEW 12:23 NCV

Have you ever tried to imagine what it might have been like to be alive when Jesus was on the earth? Can you envision walking with him, learning from him, and seeing his miracles? Most believers have thought about this. Many have wondered if it would have been easier because Jesus was right there with them.

When Jesus went away, he gave every believer a wonderful gift—the Holy Spirit! The Holy Spirit is as much God as Jesus is, and he was sent to comfort and guide us in our journey with God. In fact, Jesus says that you are more blessed than those who got to walk the earth with him because you have the Holy Spirit! Believe in his power today!

Is it easy for you to believe without seeing?

Grant

> God has proved his love by giving us his greatest treasure, the gift of his Son. And since God freely offered him up as the sacrifice for us all, he certainly won't withhold from us anything else he has to give.

ROMANS 8:32 TPT

Betsy knew how much her little sister, Emma, admired her things, but there was one toy that stood out the most— Betsy's doll. She knew it would make Emma so happy if she shared it with her, so she went down the hall to Emma's bedroom and offered it to her. Emma leapt with joy; she was so grateful that Betsy had granted her the chance to play with it. It wasn't too hard for Betsy because her love for Emma was greater than her love for any of her possessions including her doll.

Just like Betsy shared with her sister, God shared Jesus out of his great love for us. He freely gave his most valuable possession so we could be with him forever. Sometimes you may feel like God isn't granting you what you want. Remember that he always does what is best for you.

What has God granted you recently?

Compare

"There is no one holy like the Lord.
There is no God but you.
There is no Rock like our God."

1 SAMUEL 2:2 ICB

Patricia had gone on a family trip to the northern California coast. She saw so much wildlife while she was there. When she pointed out a seal to her dad, he told her it was actually a sea lion. They looked so much alike; what was the difference? Thankfully, Patricia's junior ranger book had a worksheet in it explaining the similarities and the differences between seals and sea lions.

Just like Patricia was comparing seals and sea lions, many people will say that their god is equal to the God of the Bible. In reality, there is no comparison. The God of the Bible is the one true God. He is the only living God. He is the only one to give grace to all. He is always good and kind. He is just and full of mercy. These are all qualities that belong to our God alone. There really is no comparison; our God is greater!

How does God compare to other gods?

Recall

I will praise the Lord.
I won't forget anything he does for me.

PSALM 103:2 TPT

Trina was finally old enough to be able to walk home from violin lessons on her own. Her mom had walked with her every week for a year, so she had memorized all the landmarks. Now she would recall them as she passed by: the sign at the bank with a funny joke on it meant she had to turn right, she went left at the maple tree, and right again at the library. These landmarks didn't change, and they helped Trina remember how to get home.

Just like Trina followed the landmarks to find her way home, the things God has done in your life can act like points on a map. It's important to recall the ways he has taken care of you and blessed you.

What blessings can you recall today?

Chosen

Give praise to the God and Father of our Lord Jesus Christ.
He has blessed us with every spiritual blessing. Those
blessings come from the heavenly world. They belong to
us because we belong to Christ. God chose us to belong to
Christ before the world was created. He chose us to be holy
and without blame in his eyes. He loved us.

EPHESIANS 1:3-4 NIRV

Serenity listened closely as the teacher listed off the names.
It was finally time to find out who made it into the school
choir. When her name was chosen, she felt like leaping out of
her seat. Even better, she heard her two best friends named
as well. She was so happy she was able to do something she
loved with the people she cared about.

God has chosen you as his daughter. This makes you a
daughter of the King. You are not an afterthought or a
mistake. When life is hard, remember that God made you as
one of his own—special and unique. He cares for you. These
are all truths you can cling to when you start to feel like you
aren't good enough.

How does it feel to be chosen by the Creator of the universe?

Goal

Our only goal is to please God
whether we live here or there.

2 CORINTHIANS 5:9 NCV

Rainy had big plans for her life. Her mom said she was a goal-getter. Some of her goals she could accomplish fairly quickly, like getting straight As and making the soccer team. Her long-term goals included owning her own cookie truck, traveling to Mars, and getting a pet cat. Rainy loved the feeling of checking off a goal once she accomplished it.

It's wonderful to have plans for your life. It's a good thing to accomplish your goals and mark them off lists. Most importantly, however, is to please God. If you've made plans, have you prayed about them first? Have you considered whether or not your goal glorifies God? Follow the example of Jesus and give glory to God in all you do.

How can you glorify God with your goals?

CALM

Fully awake, he rebuked the storm and shouted to the sea,
"Hush! Be still!" All at once the wind stopped howling and
the water became perfectly calm.

MARK 4:39 TPT

Soojin watched out the window as the snow swirled. Her
mom had told her this wasn't a normal snowstorm. This
was a blizzard! Mounds of snow covered the driveway,
confirming Soojin's suspicion that school would be canceled.
She felt relieved that they wouldn't have to go out in the
storm. It made her think of when Jesus calmed the storm,
and the disciples were on that boat in the middle of the sea.
She tried to imagine speaking one word and all the snow
stopping, but it seemed impossible.

Jesus calmed the wind and the waves with just one word. If
he can calm a storm, he can calm the anxiety in your heart.
Maybe you feel scared or like nothing is going your way. In
those times, ask God to help you.

What helps calm you down?

SiMPLe

"Those who are humble are happy.
The earth will belong to them."
MATTHEW 5:5 ICB

Irene's family always celebrated Christmas twice. A few weeks before Christmas, the family would go up north to Grandma's house. Grandma always knew what each member of the family wanted. This year, Irene wanted a hoverboard—and Grandma came through. She raced up and down Grandma's driveway every day for two weeks. She loved it, at least for a while. When Christmas Day came, Irene's hoverboard sat untouched in the corner of the garage. She was excited to find out what else was waiting for her under the tree at home.

The Bible tells us that true happiness doesn't come from the things that we have. This is a hard lesson for many people to learn. Those who look to material things for happiness will always be looking for more. Being content with what you have is literally a simple way to happiness.

What Makes you haPPy?

Wonderful

There were shepherds living out in the fields nearby. It was night, and they were taking care of their sheep. An angel of the Lord appeared to them. And the glory of the Lord shone around them. They were terrified. But the angel said to them, "Do not be afraid. I bring you good news. It will bring great joy for all the people. Today in the town of David a Savior has been born to you. He is the Messiah, the Lord."

LUKE 2:8-11 NIRV

Today is Christmas. It is the day we celebrate the birth of Jesus. God became a man and chose to make his home among us. Many other false gods in history were described as distant, but not our God. He chose to become a baby and to be one of us, so he could identify with us and save us.

History was forever changed with the birth of Jesus. Our lives are forever changed all these years later. Baby Jesus grew up to be a man. That man, who was still God, died on the cross for our sins so we could live forever with him. In the middle of all the gifts and fun today, it's important to pause and acknowledge our wonderful God.

What amazes you the most about Jesus coming to earth?

Breathtaking

How could I be silent when it's time to praise you?
Now my heart sings out, bursting with joy—
a bliss inside that keeps me singing,
"I can never thank you enough!"

PSALM 30:12 TPT

Blaire got off the ski lift and skied over to the top of the hill. This was one of her favorite spots. She had been skiing this hill since she was little. On clear days, she could see the city spread out in the distance. It was so beautiful to her. She breathed a quick prayer of thanks to God and then took off down the hill.

What is the most breathtaking thing you have ever seen? A sunset over the ocean? The blooming flowers in your backyard? Whatever it is, God is more amazing than the most beautiful scene you have ever gazed upon. We won't fully get it until we see him face-to-face, but for now, we enjoy the reflections of the tiny pieces of his beauty reflected all around us.

What beautiful scene has left you speechless?

Inside

"Don't look at how handsome Eliab is or how tall he is, because I have not chosen him. God does not see the same way people see. People look at the outside of a person, but the LORD looks at the heart."

1 SAMUEL 16:7 NCV

Julia kept flipping through the pages of the magazine. Every page had a girl with shiny hair, perfect make-up, and the most stylish clothes. Julia sighed because she looked nothing like the girls in those photos. Even though the magazine was full of tips and tricks on how to look a certain way, Julia knew her twisted curls and thrift-store clothes would never measure up. As her aunt entered the room, she snatched the magazine out of Julia's hands. "Don't compare yourself to them!" she said to Julia. "Remember that what is most important to God is your heart, and you, kid, have a heart of gold. You love God, you serve other people, and you're always kind. That is true beauty."

Julia knew her aunt was right. It didn't matter if she would never look like the girls in the magazine. She knew she was cherished and loved by God because of who she was, not because of how she looked.

How do you look on the inside?

Exalted

In that glorious day, you will say to one another, "Give thanks to the Lord and ask him for more! Tell the world about all that he does! Let them know how magnificent he is!" Sing praises to the Lord, for he has done marvelous wonders, and let his fame be known throughout the earth!

ISAIAH 12:4-5 TPT

Rose blushed at all the praise her grandpa was giving her. He kept bragging to anyone at his church who would listen. She was a little shy, but it felt nice, like she was truly, individually, noticed. She enjoyed hearing his compliments.

To exalt someone is to draw attention to them, and to make others take notice. Rose's grandpa had people take notice of her good qualities by speaking about them. We are told to exalt Jesus. Sometimes we want to take credit for our best qualities and accomplishments, but the praise should really go to God. Instead of making your own name famous, find ways to exalt the name of Jesus.

How can you exalt Jesus today?

Fascinating

Be in awe before his majesty.
Be in awe before such power and might!
Come worship wonderful Yahweh,
arrayed in all his splendor,
bowing in worship as he appears in the beauty of holiness.
Give him the honor due his name.

PSALM 29:2 TPT

It was the shortest day of the year and a cold, clear night. Maeve had never seen so many stars. The sky was dotted with hundreds of brilliant little lights. It made her think about how far away they were and how God knew each of them by name. She was fascinated by what the stars communicated about God.

Creation can lead us to worship God. It can cause us to seek him more. You can choose to be busy and distracted your whole life, or you can choose to notice the thousands of fascinating ways God is trying to get your attention. Spend a life in wonder of God, and you will have spent your life well.

What in God's creation do you find fascinating?

Model

Do what is good. Set an example for them in everything.
When you teach, be honest and serious. No one can question
the truth. So teach what is true. Then those who oppose you
will be ashamed. That's because they will have nothing bad
to say about us.

TITUS 2:7-8 NIRV

Summer was so annoyed at her little sister. Everything
Summer did, her sister copied. She wanted to do her own
thing without a constant shadow. Summer told her mom all
about her frustrations. Her mom reminded her that, as the
oldest sister, she held an important position. She was setting
an example for her little sister, and so far, her mom was
proud of that example. It could be frustrating at times, but it
meant her sister really admired her.

You are an example to others, and sometimes you don't even
know it! What behaviors are you modeling? Are you leading
others to Christ or away from him? Ask God to help you find
good examples and mentors so you can learn from them too.

How well are you modeling the character of Jesus?

Belong

You are a chosen people, royal priests, a holy nation,
a people for God's own possession. You were chosen to
tell about the wonderful acts of God, who called you
out of darkness into his wonderful light.

1 PETER 2:9 NCV

Karen's family was not traditional. She had been adopted out
of the foster care system along with her seven other siblings.
None of them were related by blood, and all of them had
different ethnicities and ages. Her parents also took care of
their elderly aunt. Karen loved her family because of this.
Her parents gave everyone a sense of belonging. No matter
where they came from, they were family because they were
together.

Do you ever feel like you don't belong? You are a part of a
special, chosen group. You are one of God's children! You
belong to the family of God. In this family, you are valued,
your talents are needed, and you are loved.

What makes you feel like you belong?